AT THE LOCH
OF THE GREEN CORRIE

Andrew Greig is the author of six acclaimed books of poetry, two Himalayan mountaineering expedition books, and several novels including *That Summer*, *When They Lay Bare*, *In Another Light* (Scottish Book of the Year) and *Romanno Bridge*. His last non-fiction book, *Preferred Lies*, is already seen as a contemporary classic. A full-time writer, he lives in Orkney and Edinburgh with his wife, the novelist Lesley Glaister.

'Should you ever find yourself in need of some explanations as to why Scots are the way they are. Why Scotland looks the way it does. How the geology of the country is as important to the history of the country as the lists of tartan clad nobility might be. Why the profundity steeped in a pseudo simplicity gifted to us by Hogg, Ferguson, and Burns, marches inexorably forward in a culture which seems to be able to weather the most intolerable strains impressed on it by modern media types. If you have a desire to luxuriate in the most beautiful use of the English language borne along by the love of one gifted poet for a recognized master of melancholy, then this is the book for you. It most certainly is the book for me.'
Billy Connolly

'A ruminative, beautifully written book that is at once a biography of MacCaig, an account of a journey in North West Scotland and a captivating memoir of Greig's life as a poet, Himalayan climber and fisherman.'
Sunday Times

'The recounting of [his] journey is a triumph. That this book is written by a poet is immediately obvious – the language is richly evocative, but is handled with lightness and delicacy. The balance of Greig's tone is simply perfect. This is a lovely book. Many, I suspect, will want to return to it again and again. It is like a rare malt whiskey: poignant, smoky and with a taste that makes you think of many great and important things.'
Alexander McCall Smith

'It is clearly a quest, but for what? It is a pilgrimage, but to where? A homage, but to whom? This beautiful book seems at first to lay bare its own answers. It is a love song to a writer, to Scotland, to a transfiguring landscape.'
Scotland on Sunday

'It is completely absorbing ... and the intense self-scrutiny is matched by landscape writing worthy of Stevenson himself. Over and over, Greig makes place into an event in its own right.'
Guardian

'Painfully honest, beautifully written, it is a writer's way of processing the world.'
The Scotsman

'Consistently well-written, sometimes dazzlingly so ... [it's] a considered, quietly ecstatic act of tribute.'
Independent

'Within a few feet of the ascent towards the Green Corrie I realised I'd follow this man just about anywhere ... Be warned – this is one of those books that will annoy whoever is sitting next to you. If you're anything like me you won't be able to resist saying "Listen – listen to this!"'
Scottish Sunday Herald

'Like another of Greig's previous books, *Preferred Lies*, which was ostensibly about golf, it is a personal and sensitive rumination in which the author reviews his life, his family, friendships and affairs.'
Times Literary Supplement

'The narrative is enriched by thoughtful reflections on everything from the history of geology to the nature of Scottishness. And through this beguiling mix runs the thread of Norman MacCaig's view of Assynt through his stories and poems. As in all the best fishing books we learn nothing about catching fish. We learn a lot about Greig and something about fishing in wild places. This is a compelling book.'
Trout and Salmon

'Tribute to a great poet and friend, celebration of home and autobiography, this is a moving and richly atmospheric book about life's adventure.'
The Herald

'An original and beautifully wrought meditation on life, nature and friendship set against the wild backdrop of the north-west Highlands.'
Country Life

'This richly atmospheric narrative is a remarkable piece of writing.'
The Good Book Guide

'Rarely maudlin but sometimes bleak, the writing suggests a need for healing: occasionally Greig seems like a Fisher King shoring up fragments, trying to set the landscape in order. It is beautifully done.'
Literary Review

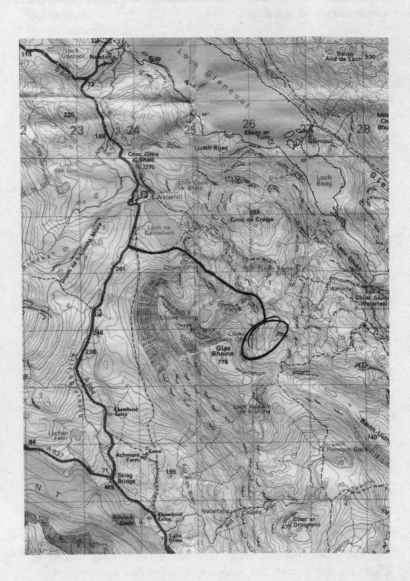

AT THE LOCH
OF THE GREEN
CORRIE

Andrew Greig

First published in Great Britain in 2010 by Quercus
This paperback edition published in 2011 by

Quercus
21 Bloomsbury Square
London
WC1A 2NS

A CIP catalogue record for this book is available
from the British Library

ISBN 978 0 85738 136 1

10 9 8 7 6 5 4 3

Text designed and typeset by Ellipsis

Printed and bound in Great Britain by Clays Ltd. St Ives plc.

To Norman and his pals

For Lesley and mine

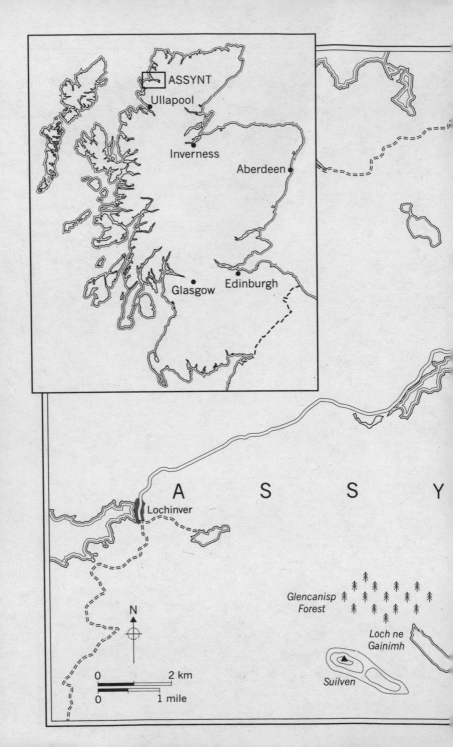

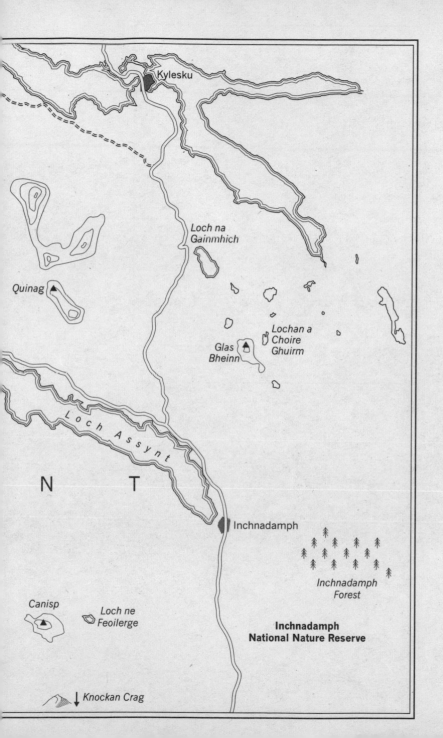

A rough pronunciation guide

Suilven — as *sool-ven*

Glas Bheinn — as *glass vine*

Quinag — as *Koon yak*

Lochan a Choire Ghuirm — something like *ghirim* but the
first i is like a cross halfway between *oo* and the i in *hit*

Loch Dubh Meallan Mhurchaidh — *loch doo meeyalan voorichee*

Loch na Gainmhich — *loch na ganiveech*

Loch na Faoleige — *loch ni fi-leegi*

Bealach a Bhuirich — as *bee-a-loch a voorich*

Gaedhealtachd or Gaeltachd — *gale-tack* (first vowel l-o-n-g,
as per Sorley MacLean)

Note that emphasis in Gaelic nearly always comes on the
first syllable, thus *GANiveech* etc.

A CHARGE IS LAID

'Man is in love and loves what vanishes'

Were it merely a matter of *digging*, I would not choose to exhume the dead, nor live again the time we went to fish for the old poet and his friends. I would not ask you whose days on Earth are numbered as mine, to come along as audience, witnesses, companions of the heart.

Behind the journey to Lochinver I made that day there lay another. Five years earlier I walked down a familiar tenement street to press the buzzer and ascend the worn stone stairs to call on Norman MacCaig, native of Edinburgh, poet of Assynt. It was to be the last time we talked alone together, and that night he would lay on me the charge by which I now remember him.

Dim in here, smelling of food, stone, smoke. As I fit my shoe into the hollow at the centre of each step, I am thinking of all the hands that have tugged at this wooden banister. A phantom pantheon of poets come trooping up these winding stairs, clinking with carry-outs from the Abbotsford or Milnes Bar, still laughing and smoking, the foggy brewery

1

guff of 1950s Edinburgh clinging to their tweedy jackets. They are ready to continue the party, the jousting, gossip, laughter, flyting.

Norman of course leads; lean, upright, classical head held high, he stalks up those stairs like a heron. Behind him, murmuring a Gaelic lament under his breath, comes Sorley MacLean, then Goodsir Smith the clown, mimicking a rival's latest pomposity. MacDiarmid puts his surprisingly small hand on the banister to pull himself up after young Crichton Smith, visiting from Oban. At the rear, nervously clutching beer bottles under his brown corduroy jacket, comes lantern-jawed Mackay Brown, followed by Alexander Scott trying to hone a remark by which the evening will be remembered. Tom Scott the tormented Marxist is elsewhere, pounding the wet streets in his duffel coat, in search of the beloved of at least three of that company . . .

All gone now, though the hollow their feet made resides in this stone, darkly glinting as a pencil's lead. Their work remains, though I think sometimes MacCaig would have given all his poems for one more day's fishing, or another evening session with his friends. I am glad that bargain was not his to make.

On the landing I look back down the winding stair of memory. A nervous, excited East Fife schoolboy has come to call on the legendary poet. In his Mod jacket and chisel-toed, elastic-sided Chelsea boots, he is hurrying up these stairs to hear the verdict on his aspirations, cheerfully oblivious of the poets he passes through. My young, skinny self is right behind me as I reach the mat and raise my hand – which bears its first brown splotches – to chap on that worn door.

'I should like you to fish for me at the Loch of the Green Corrie,' MacCaig concludes over our final dram. 'Only it's not called that. But if you go to Lochinver and ask for a man called Norman MacAskill, *if* he likes you he *may* tell you where it is. If you catch trout, I shall be delighted. And if you fail, then looking down from a place in which I do not believe, I shall be *most amused*.'

He shuffles with me to his door. We shake hands, his grip painfully bony.

There comes a point when goodnight may well be goodbye. At the turn of the tenement stair I look back. He is still standing in his doorway and I see one more time the high forehead, those arrow-head cheekbones and smoke-white plume of hair, the deep-set, watchful, mournful eyes – he'd been a strikingly fine-looking man and not unaware of it when he'd stalked upright through the bars and streets of Edinburgh. The sardonic mouth twitches, his right hand comes up, waves once.

'Ta-ta.'

That was the last evening I spent alone with Norman MacCaig. At his funeral months later, sitting among writer friends, each with our own memories of the man, looking down at the box that contained the mortal remains of one who once contained all Assynt, I remembered his last words to me. Nothing grand or clever, just 'Ta-ta'. How very Norman – at once childlike and concise: *thank you* and *goodnight* in one. He relished economy and clarity, did MacCaig.

At the end of the service, after the praises of the man, the friend and the poet, praises that would have at once amused, gratified and embarrassed him, the heartbreaking slow fiddle air of Aly Bain broke into a celebratory reel. Time to go.

Outside were many faces I knew, mostly of my generation. The grand old men were nearly all gone. But there was Sorley MacLean in the sunshine by the tombstones, looking rather well and cheery. My father had been the same towards the end of his long life: outlived another one! I wasn't at that stage yet; death of friends just brought chill and sorrow.

We shook hands and before too many people had gathered I asked 'Sorley, what would the Gaelic be for *Loch of the Green Corrie?*'

Sorley MacLean, last of the Gaelic bards, with still nine months to live, never had MacCaig's concision. By the time he'd rubbed his stubby grey moustache, frowned and nodded, drawn many syllables from the words 'Well, now . . .', family and friends were upon us.

I would have to go to Lochinver and ask for Norman MacAskill and hope he likes me. For the charge had been set: to find and fish the Loch of the Green Corrie, Norman MacCaig's most loved place in all his beloved Assynt, the ruinous, transcendent heartland of the North West Highlands of Scotland.

Were it just a matter of digging, down through hard ground and hard history, I would not revisit that time. It is hard enough to attend to today. Hard to stay alert to our partners and friends, to children, work, the daily pleasures and necessities of our lives, even as they slip away.

Not long ago my beloved sat letting sand sift through her fingers onto a North Ronaldsay beach, as though she herself were a neat-waisted hourglass time ran through. She saw me watching, smiled ruefully then clasped my bare arm with still-gritty, still-warm fingers. We did not need to speak of what we accepted then.

Our days are numbered and we still don't know what that number is. So let us not sift through the dead who grow more numerous every year. Let the book of homage remain unwritten and unread.

Yet there are places and times on this Earth when the ground as it were grows thin, and the dead arise of themselves. Gone days, dead parents, lost friends, old loves, rise round us as an escort, an entourage, to provoke, counsel and console. As we drive, or lie with a book at the day's end, we may glimpse them at the edge of vision. They must be spoken with, if we are to remain honest.

Without digging or summoning, absences rise quivering like midges over bracken, like heat-haze over a Highland road – the A835, for instance, west of Altguish, as I drive it in late May. They move along with me as I turn the wheel, and lift my eyes to see again Suilven's sandstone dome raise, above the village of Lochinver, its monumental correlative of Norman MacCaig's forehead.

It is not nostalgia, this feeding on air as certain plants do. It seems our roots are in the invisible.

So many summers

Beside one loch, a hind's neat skeleton,
Beside another, a boat pulled high and dry:
Two neat geometries drawn in the weather:
Two things already dead and still to die.

I passed them every summer, rod in hand,
Skirting the bright blue or the spitting grey,
And, every summer, saw how the bleached timbers
Gaped wider and the neat ribs fell away.

Time adds one malice to another one –
Now you'd look very close before you knew
If it's the boat that ran, the hind went sailing.
So many summers, and I have lived them too.

Norman MacCaig

Day 1

Cast: going West

When I go, I'd like my sign-off to be even briefer than Norman's last goodnight: *Ta*.

For as the car hums over Drumochter in radiant late May, despite everything it is thanks I want to give again. Much has happened in the four years since Norman died; now I am finally on my way to a rendezvous in Ullapool.

The car is stashed with bulging rucksack, maps, boots, carrier bags, waterproofs, tent, sleeping bag, stove. My rod is propped in the seat beside me, wedged in with landing net and boxes of lines, reels, trout flies. It twitches as I drive, my slender nodding passenger.

When I cleared the gear from the glory hole yesterday, the old lines and casts were tangled – how do they do that? – and the hooks were the colour of old blood. In truth I am not much of a fisherman, an apprentice at best, and I haven't fished for ages. The friend who taught me how to, who should have been with me on this ploy, died a year ago on Everest, in his tent with a book across his chest.

I still wonder: which book?

Mal Duff is gone. For nearly ten years he enlarged my life, dragging me into Scottish winter climbing en route to three Himalayan expeditions, on the Mustagh Tower, Everest North East Ridge and Lhotse Shar. In our times off the hills, he introduced me to his other passion: fly fishing. We fished together, not so many times that I don't remember each one of them.

If I hadn't fished with Mal, I never would have mentioned it to Norman, for fishing to become our principal subject of conversation whenever we met, leading to his final request. So the line runs out and settles on me being here now, descending the A9 past the signs to Culloden – let us put old defeats behind us for today! – towards Inverness, its glinting bridges and dolphin-torn estuary.

What is this love, this profound and absolute attachment I feel for Scotland? Why do these mottled rising green-brown hills, these humped fields, this river, even the familiar cast of the houses, feel so right and move me so? Lesley accepts that she is English, but it is not a defining fact for her, any more than being right-handed or blue-eyed. Whereas she can see that for me being Scottish is fundamental to who I am.

As I turn off at the Tore roundabout onto the A835 to Ullapool, drive on past scattered villages where the valley pushes a green wedge between the hills on either side, I'm thinking of one of MacCaig's shortest poems, 'Patriot'.

> My only country
> is six feet high
> and whether I love it or not
> I'll die
> for its independence.

The idea of patriotism was abhorrent to him. He'd seen enough of what it led to. He could not love an abstraction. But he loved – my God how he loved! – things that were solid, concrete, particular: some people, dogs, frogs, rivers, mountains, toads, a wild rose bush, so many kinds of birds. His vision was earthly, corporeal.

That last evening at Norman's, he'd been talking about fishing in Assynt. He flicked his thumb over a tiny badge on the lapel of his tweed jacket. *AAA*.

'Nothing to do with motorcars or alcoholics,' he said drily. 'This is the honour of which I am most proud.'

'More than the OBE?'

He giggled, the air hissing through his teeth. MacCaig was fortunate, his brain was good to the end. But in his last years at times the old man moved aside to let the child he'd once been peek out at you. It was in the giggle, the mischief, the love of expressions like *ta-ta*.

'Much more. Some people whose good opinion I cherish made me an honorary life member of the Assynt Anglers Association.'

But his legs – circulatory and heart problems, acerbated by constant smoking – had become so bad he could no longer fish in his favourite lochs. He hadn't been able to for years. He lapsed into silence, sipped his whisky. His face had sunk, leaving the jutting cheekbones, high eye-sockets arched over the watchful, lustrous eyes. Norman could drink whisky and converse all night and never appear drunk or tired. Now he looked lost. Since his wife Isabel died five years earlier, these silences came more often.

Maybe that was why I had asked, in one of those confidences that come after midnight with drink taken, just the two of us in high-backed armchairs near the fire, 'Norman, what is your favourite spot in the world?'

He blinked himself back from wherever he'd been.

'Assynt,' he said. How much love and memory he freighted into that one word.

'I know it's Assynt!' I said. 'But *where* in Assynt? Your favourite place?'

He took his time. Another drink, another drag of the cigarette.

'I think it would have to be the Loch of the Green Corrie. Only it's not called that. AK and I used to fish there.' His head turned towards a black and white photo on his mantelpiece. An eager-looking man stands outside a church; in dark suit and tie, hands on hips, he confronts the camera with an air of brimming mischief: AK MacLeod, mourned in wonderful, desolate elegies. 'It's many years since I've been there. It's remote, you see, high up in the hills and quite a scramble. I think about it a lot.'

And that was when he set the charge that has brought us here. 'In fact, I should like you to go and fish there for me.'

He leaned forward and tapped me on the knee.

'I loved that man!' he said vehemently. 'Not like *that*, you understand, but I loved him.'

I drive through Garve, then past the junction where one road goes off to Achnasheen, the red-ledged towers of

Torridon and the hills of Kishorn. Pass those names across your tongue as though they were poems, as though they were whisky. These names and places have histories for me, dating from childhood holidays, my father's tobacco-rasped voice offering fragments of anecdotes as his gloved hands turned the big wheel of our Humber Hawk. He claimed to have driven every numbered road in Scotland; each had memories and associations for him.

Accelerating straight on up Strath Garve, my heart rises with the road. The landscape is empty now, any house or car an event, the hills all-surrounding, the river flashing brown and clear over stones. I wind the window down to check the air: moist sweetness with underlying acidic peat.

I have entered the West.

Retrieve: a Scots Pine

Off to the left, on a lee slope above the burn, stood a solitary Scots Pine. Some love the rowan, the mountain ash of good fortune, with its bloody beads shimmering. The oak, silver birch, copper beech, all are noble and useful and have their adherents. The Scots Pine is mine.

On impulse I stopped and got out of my useful mobile cage, walked across the moor. I ran my palm over the rough red-brown plates of the bark, leaned in to sniff its resinous heart. I looked up at the blasted, twisted branches, some dead, others still passing energy into that enduring core.

My brother the forester talks of the 'character' of tree species. Each has its own encoded shape, the way it will grow, its final height, even its natural life span. All very determinist. But Sandy also demonstrated how that shape is affected by circumstance: a plantation of Scots Pine, close-planted, will stand thin and slim and straight, good for telegraph poles. That shape is in response to proximity. Whereas my image of the archetypal Scots Pine is like this one: stumpy, twisted, with big horizontal branches, the rough trunk glowing as though lit by a distant fire. Enduring, thrawn, tough, inelegant, solitary . . .

The very image of my father, who first named it for me. He was not good at trees, but this one he named as something special, as though it mattered to him.

I sat down at the base of the tree, leaned back against it

and looked down the glaciated, deserted valley. Some people signify in our lives, even though we do not see them often. Indubitably and mysteriously, Norman MacCaig was some kind of father figure for me. He was something and he represented something.

Urbane, elegant, subtle, caustic, an intimidating, welcoming man alert with laughter and increasingly informed by sorrow and loss – had Norman been a tree, in his latter years, after the deaths of AK and Goodsir Smith, Chris Grieve and then his wife Isabel, he would have been an elegant, wounded silver birch. On that last evening we had together, in pauses he looked ancient and lost. And then the quip, the delighted grin.

'You've heard that one before? Well, I am in my *anecdotage*!' Hissing giggle. 'And have I said that before?'

But now I was leaning against something of my real father. He was at my back, as he always has been since his death some fifteen years ago. It is he I have yet to make a full reckoning with, that powerful, difficult, armoured man, so shaped by his circumstances – the two world wars, his drive and his sensitivity to slights, the friends who died young, his early poverty and lost loves. With my old man you could see the snapped branches, the broken crown, feel the force and cost of his endurance. He was of a generation who learned not to feel what they felt, and took some pride in that.

Then I had it, the scrap of story which had made me stop here.

It began as a yarn about how he and his classmates, in the early years of the last century, would challenge each other to walk for as long as possible carrying a penny gripped between thumb and forefinger, the arm hanging down. *It may seem an easy thing to do, laddie, but no matter how hard you try, sooner or later it will drop.* Muscular fatigue, numbness, something like that. And I thought: what a fantastically futile thing to do, and how deep and Scottish a teaching it must have been, yoking together money, endurance, and the inevitability of loss.

Then my father went on to say how, still carrying his penny, as a boy he once stopped in a gale under a Scots Pine. He stood against it, thrilled − not a word he had much use for − to feel bark shift against his back. He said he'd imagined the tree a mast, and yearned to be sailing where that wind was blowing, far from Arbroath, out of Scotland, beyond Europe, to a blue space on his father's globe. *The South China Seas. I aye wanted to see them.*

And in his twenties, he did. Penang, Sumatra, Borneo, Java, he knew them, lived and worked and loved there. If not for a woman, I think he would have stayed there. I think exile would have suited him, as it suited his brothers who all fled their impoverished, wounded country.

We arrive at who we are first by following, then by divergence. I am not my father, nor Norman MacCaig. Sitting under that tree off the road to Ullapool, I realised my business is not to carry money till it drops, and my drive is not for exile. The myrtle-laden breeze passed over my face, but I did not yearn to follow where it was going to. My predilection has always been, will always be, to sit until I sense the source, the place the wind comes from.

Cast: towards a rendezvous

It's been a few years since I've been this way, climbing with a lover and friend into the rough bounds of Wester Ross. But that was before Lesley, before good people got hurt for this chance at happiness, before I didn't die, back when Mal and Norman and Sorley were still alive, and my mother's memory could be relied on.

I pull up at Loch Glascarnoch, turn off the engine and get out. Walk up and down. If someone loves you more whole-heartedly than you love them, in the end you, not they, are the poorer. In her grace and dignity, my friend always knew that.

The water is flat calm, a pure metallic blue, holding a perfect inverted Tom Ban Mor without movement. The mountain going up and the mountain going down articulate at the rust-brown hinge of the far shore. A certain smell travels from the back of my nose to the core of the brain: bog myrtle. I hunker down, pluck a few coarse matt blue-green leaves, crush them under my nose and feel dizzy. This is the smell of childhood summer, the otherness of the West, a world wrapped in a scent.

The road is silent, not a car, bird, voice. Nothing stirs in this long, flooded glen. I sometimes feel I did die sixteen months ago, on a hospital trolley in Sheffield, while the pressure from the blocked ventricle squeezed my brain to half its normal size, and since then I've come back intermittently to haunt myself. There are worse places to haunt than Wester Ross. Norman must have come this way so many summers, by bus and then, once the family could afford it, by car. I think of him travelling, alert, withdrawn, noticing, eager to see his dearest place and friends again.

What will remain of him and AK in the Green Corrie?

I flick away the silent, burning view like a cigarette and drive on for Altguish, Corrieshalloch Gorge, Loch Broom, Inverlael and Ullapool, the lovely names of Wester Ross. As it happens there is gold in the streams of my country's hills. In a burn in the Cairngorms I have seen the pan swirl and sift as memory does, till the residue shines.

Somewhere out there is the glen where Lesley and I sat down on our first walk together, and talked casually about insects, novels, family, music, everything but what had grown between us. I opened my mouth, found myself saying 'My heart is thumping, because I so want to kiss you,' and she turned to me, and my life, like a diverted stream, began to run into a new channel.

Where will it go, what are we going to do with it? With me in Orkney much of the time, and her in Sheffield with her work and children, our lives are semi-detached. We are together but we are often not. We don't talk about the future beyond the short-term.

I put the foot down on the descent to Loch Broom, shimmering blue-white under the overhead midsummer sun. This road is now so wide, fast and smooth that I've just gone from the east to the west coast of Scotland in an hour. It is utterly changed from the romantic but laborious single-track road we used to drive with my father in the late Fifties. Stirling to Lochinver took us eleven hours then, including two ferries: a real journey, into a very different world, one that looked, smelled, sounded quite unlike Lowland Scotland.

Different too since the last time I came this way is the car I'm driving. This May noon finds me barrelling alongside Loch Broom in a six-year-old Audi 80, and though I've never cared about motor cars, I'm enjoying this one, the way it sits on the road through corners, the gear change smooth as political tongues.

Into Ullapool at the top of the loch, an unusually tidy and regular village for the Highlands. The name is Norse: *Ulli's farm*. Loch Broom used to host huge red-rusted Russian factory ships, and their presence added a certain frisson to Ullapool life in the days of the Iron Curtain.

They've gone now. Times, lovers, political geography and art forms have changed. Whenever we met, Norman would say 'Not writing *prose* I hope, Mr Greig?' For years I could reassure him. But after a certain point life presents itself not so much as a mosaic of lyric moments as the unfolding of one thing after another, that is to say *a story*. And a good story can buy a motor car.

The Audi glides along the front street, turns up then stops outside the Ceilidh Place. I get out, the car door shuts with a satisfyingly solid yet muted *thunk*, like the close of a well-cadenced paragraph.

I love that word, *rendezvous*, so freighted with possible adventure. The Dorward brothers are sitting at a table in dazzling midday sun, each with a pint. They wave. Crossing the road, I feel light, unburdened. The age of poetry is not entirely ended. Flecks of it still glitter in the pauses between stories, among the mud and gravel bed of the stream.

Here we go.

Retrieve: 'There are no swear words in the Gaelic'

We shook hands. Perhaps if we'd met up in Edinburgh or London, we might have hugged. But somehow not in Ullapool.

No, here it was firm handshakes, delighted smile from Andy and grin from Peter, a quick glance into the eyes of old friends. Twenty years earlier an enthusiastic dark-haired youth came up to me after a reading and exclaimed 'I really like your poetry!' A promising start to a lasting friendship. Last time I'd seen Andy was in New York, when Lesley and I stayed at his apartment in Greenwich Village. On that visit I was still weak and shaky from hospital after head trauma, coping intermittently, just hanging on.

'You look a lot better, Greigy!'

'I feel it. Thanks for coming.'

'Fishing for MacCaig? Wouldn't have missed this for the world!'

'We can always go on a sodden fifty-mile yomp across nowhere next year,' Peter added.

It had been a while since I'd seen Peter. After returning tanned and thin from two years of aid work in Bolivia and Nicaragua, life had changed gear for the young boy racer. Now he was a GP in a practice in London, had two small children Jack and Jamie with his partner Deborah, and we met only a couple of times a year. For a long time I knew and thought of him as 'Andy's wee brother'. Now a man with family, he looked if anything slightly older than Andy – leaner, more edgy, weathered.

We went back into the Ceilidh Place for a quick drink and lunch. The bar was loud with a swarm of men with Seventies hair and sideburns and big sweaters. At first we thought they were foreign. Then I recognised a few familiar words, and caught the tell-tale *sshing* of the 's', looked at the sideburns and the built-up shoes.

'These are very drunk Lewismen,' I said confidently.

They informed everyone in earshot that they were waiting to catch the ferry back to Stornaway. There'd been one yesterday, but they had missed it because someone was too drunk and got lost. And they'd missed it the day before that, because, well they couldn't quite remember why. But they'd probably definitely catch this one, so long as they got a few more rounds in first.

We got our food and went outside. Two of them swayed out and headed down the street, now speaking Gaelic.

Ten years earlier I'd been on Skye during a key shinty match: Portree v Kingussie. Clouds down, rain calamitous – an average Skye day. The pitch was churned to No Man's Land by large and very muddy young men wielding hockey sticks like clubs, swiping with great skill and abandon at a flying ball. Most team games have their roots in warfare or fertility rituals – shinty dispenses with the fertility part.

As impressive were the spectators standing all round the pitch, ankle-deep in mud, stoically enduring the rain with the help of little flasks passing hand to hand. Among them I saw Sorley MacLean. Gaeldom's greatest living poet, small and plump in an old coat and battered hat.

'And how are your family?' he asked courteously, as he always did. Then we turned our attention back to the shinty. He was shaking with excitement, up on his toes as Portree pressed forward, flinging his arms out in disgust at a missed chance, howling at a bone-jarring tackle on one of his team, applauding another immediately inflicted by the same player.

He had been a keen player in his youth, up to the troubled time when he wrote the towering *Poems to Eimhir* that yoked a tragic and complicated love affair to an anguished awareness of the Spanish Civil War. Clearly the inner fires burned still for shinty, and probably for the international brotherhood of men and women.

I noticed that though the conversation around me was in Gaelic, the curses, rants and imprecations were all pitched in the short, direct terms that Low Dutch imported into English to such forceful effect. I remarked on this to Sorley. He considered the matter then chuckled. Raindrops showered from his hat brim, his stubby grey moustache shivered water.

'There are no swear words in the Gaelic,' he said, then paused. Sorley was a great man for the pauses. Not, you sensed, because his thoughts were slow, but because they had many ramifications. 'At least, no short ones.'

Cast: in search of a man who may tell you

As we transferred their packs and fishing tackle into my car, I noticed how limited were the food supplies Andy and Peter had brought for this ploy.

'Oh, we've got plenty,' Andy said confidently.

Andy is good at easy, reassuring confidence. That, along with a clear, quick mind and boundless enthusiasm, was why he'd done so well in the printing business. He'd say firmly in his East Coast Scottish accent 'The name's Dorward, Andrew Dorward,' hold out his hand, and people believed whatever he said next. How could you doubt a man who sounded like Sean Connery without the slight speech impediment?

Still, I'd known Andy for some twenty years and learned his nature paints a gloss on things, so I enquired further. It seemed the Dorward boys intended we live for four days on porridge, cheese, tea – and fish, if we caught enough.

And drink?

'We've got a bottle of Glenmorangie!' Andy said proudly.

'*One* bottle? For four nights!! And what about wine?'

In the store in the street behind the Ceilidh Place we stocked up with real food. I basketed chocolate, bacon, eggs, sausages, plenty oatcakes and nibbly stuff to have with the extra whisky, potatoes, soups, beans, biscuits. They soon got the idea and we converged at the check-out with some heartening duplications, especially on the wine and whisky front.

'Greigy, you are such a pig!' Andy chortled (he really does chortle; sometimes he even says *chortle chortle*).

'It's time to put aside our Protestant heritage,' I said. 'Suffering and deprivation are *not* good for the soul. Pleasure, however, is.'

As Andy put our provisions through, Peter admitted that in the past on their annual marathon treks he and Andy had striven to outdo each other in privation, carrying ever-heavier loads greater distances with less food and poorer clothing. Partly because they had less money back then, partly just the principle of the thing.

'But you must have had it tough on your Himalayan expeditions, Greigy.'

'I learned something on those trips,' I said firmly, taking up a clinking bag. 'Never make things harder than they have to be.'

Now properly equipped, we left Ullapool to the Lewismen and took the A835 to Lochinver, in search of a man called Norman MacAskill.

A twisting descent into Lochinver, the road a tarmac stream swerving down through little rowan and birch trees, binary sunlight streaming on/off codes through the leaves. Andy and Peter are in high spirits – their default mode, especially for Andy – debating how many fish they are going to catch, the technicalities of flies, line weight, hook size. I'm buoyant, because my heart lifts at the word *Lochinver*. It began with childhood holidays, on our way to the pale, haunted sands of nearby Achmelvich – you can hear the little breakers collapse and withdraw when you voice it: *Achmelvich*.

After my father retired, he did locums in Lochinver when the regular GP went on holiday. He took us off school and we spent extended Easter holidays here. As we enter the village I indicate the solid stone house on the left: that was the doctor's house, that's where we stayed.

The doctor had a little West Highland terrier that accompanied us into the hills. *Spec* he was called. Gaelic for wasp. Certainly he buzzed around, whizzing through heather on his stumpy, indefatigable legs. Dear God, that must be forty years ago. The doctor is long dead, my father too. Spec's bones lie in that garden.

But Suilven, that improbable, totemic mountain, remains. A Norse–Gaelic hybrid name: *Sula Bheinn*, 'pillar mountain', its great dome rears over the village. From this side Suilven is bare red rock rising like a colossal old-fashioned beehive. Follow up the rushing Kirkaig burn and Suilven becomes a long mountain like an exaggerated dolphin: great bulging head, spine falling to a narrow col, then rising to a sharp fishtail at the east end.

I park the car near the bridge over the Inver, and we step out into the near-empty village. In a commitment to following MacCaig's instructions, I haven't tried to contact Norman MacAskill in advance, and there is no guarantee he still lives here. Or that he is still alive. Some five years have passed since MacCaig made his request, and these were all elderly men.

I might have dragged Andy and Peter here for nothing.

Without MacAskill we won't find the Loch of the Green Corrie ('Only it's not called that'). There are a hundred other lochs to fish in Assynt, but only one has brought us here.

They look at me expectantly. I contemplate the Tourist Information, then notice along from it there's a butcher shop with the sign *A. MacAskill*.

'Wait here.'

The street is in a sun-washed daze. Here's the bakery where the child-me was sent for morning rolls. The smell of them in chilly mornings, scent and warmth rising through the brown paper bag as I hurried home, anticipating breakfast, my world at once secure and novel. Now it is neither.

In the butcher shop I ask for a man named Norman MacAskill. I get lucky, they know him well though he's not a relative. He lives in that house off the end of the street, down there. I might find him in.

Feeling like three hired assassins in a spaghetti Western, we stroll down the street towards the house. I hate cold-calling people. I'm no journalist. I've got to make him like me. He might not be in.

'It's probably better you wait here,' I say.

I open through the little gate and ring the bell. Nothing happens. I ring again, wait some more. As I look back at Andy and Peter, the door opens behind me.

'Yes?'

'Are you Norman MacAskill?'

'Yes.'

'I've come to see you because of Norman MacCaig.'

He stares at me, blinking.

'Norman is dead.'

'That's why I've come.'

I am inspected for a long time. Norman MacAskill is elderly, quite stocky but not tall, wearing a tweed jacket and wool tie indoors. He also seems suspicious, testy, wary. I begin to understand MacCaig's '*If* he likes you.'

'You'd best come in,' he says grudgingly.

I wave back to the Dorwards and go inside.

Retrieve: 'Perhaps you should write some like your own'

The first thing I ever made was a song, about the Summer Isles, near Achiltibuie. It was short and simple as my life at that point. Wild foaming horses would not drag it from me now, but aged seven I sang it for hours in the car as we drove along the single-track roads of Wester Ross and Assynt. Eventually it was suggested I sang it out the window.

With the window wound full down, I sat out on the sill, holding on to the roof rack, the warm hill-and-sea-smelling air sweeping over my arms. It would seem wildly irresponsible now, to have a child sit halfway out the car, but the roads were near-empty and my father unhurried. I feel still the euphoria, the song snatched from my mouth by the slipstream, and the curious dislocation when we turned a corner and saw the Summer Isles again, lying in sunlight as they so often did, and then my song about them seemed different, not quite true, because the song and the thing are not the same.

I had been thinking about that daft wee song the first time I chapped on Norman MacCaig's door, aged seventeen, keen and nervous. A few weeks earlier I had sent him my poems care of *The Scotsman*, more as a tribute than anything, a thank-you for his poems where I'd read about places I knew. A reply had come back in flowing dark ink

Come and see me. So I'd put on my brother's mohair jacket, shined my Chelsea boots and caught the bus to Leven, another bus to Edinburgh. I'd never been in the city by myself, didn't understand the bus system, so I asked and walked all the way.

Odd to calculate MacCaig must have then been the age I am now. He looked so *senior*, so upright, poised, school-masterly. I blurted that I knew Assynt too, that we'd had family holidays there, and my father had done locums for the doctor in Lochinver.

'Oh, yes? Do you know Achmelvich?'

Sweating, I nodded enthusiastically. 'We went there often. I still think about it a lot.'

'So do I,' he said, and that was that.

He spoke deliberately, making time for each word to be weighted and brushed with irony, sarcasm, tenderness. It was like words were little sweets on a tray, the tray his wife brought in after five minutes, with tea and cake. She said Hello, smiled, put down the tray and left.

Norman cleared his throat and picked up some quarto-sized sheets that I recognised. At that moment I wished I'd never sent them; I didn't have to look at my poems again to know they were inadequate. Just the fact of them in his hand made that obvious.

I have never forgotten his words, measured out, balanced and slyly nuanced as one of his poems.

'I have read your poems, Mr Greig.' *(Pause)* 'I quite like some of them.' *(Pause, flush of joy through my system)* 'But then I would, because some of them are quite like mine.'

(Pause, dismay, certain knowledge this is true) He looked up, that wolfish grin. 'Perhaps you should write some like your own. *(Pause)* This one could be – given time.'

His judgement was true, of course. I loved his poems, so I took them as a model of how poems should be. Those I'd written that weren't like his were like the other poets I'd haphazardly alighted on – Iain Crichton Smith, Miroslav Holub, Cavafy, Apollinaire, Eliot.

What he said was cutting and funny and true. It was also – I realised even then, heading home to Anstruther on the bus with my shameful imitation poems sprinkled with his notes – generous. He wasn't looking for disciples, a coterie of imitators. He offered me the best and truest challenge one can offer a young writer, after suggesting they read a whole lot more: *perhaps you should write some like your own*.

Of course, it takes years to discover where 'your own' is located. And if you ever do, it's probably time to go fish another, higher and more problematic, lochan.

Cast: a question of permission

Norman MacAskill sits down heavily in an armchair and stares at me. He doesn't ask me to take off my jacket, nor to sit down; there's no offer of tea or a dram. The culture of the Gaeltachd is subtly reserved but very polite, with politeness flowering into open-handed generosity. Hospitality is important.

But he just sits, stares and waits. Finally, uninvited, I sit down opposite him and explain about Norman's request that I fish for him and AK at the Loch of the Green Corrie. I don't include '*If* he likes you.'

Mr MacAskill is a man of few words and long silences. I wonder if he is slightly deaf. I later learned he took some pleasure in his curmudgeonly reputation. The whole trip rests on him coming up with the goods and in my anxiety I gabble somewhat. I hear my Central Belt accent, see myself as an over-eager door-stepping townie come to rip off Norman's memory.

Finally MacAskill stirs. I think he's about to offer a drink, but instead he stares at me suspiciously, as if I'm selling something. Maybe I am.

'Did you know Norman well?'

I don't want to claim an intimacy I don't have. I'd met with Norman MacCaig maybe a couple of dozen times over thirty-five years; visited him at home on occasion; had some evenings out in pubs, usually in company; shared a few readings with him. He'd refereed applications for me, read through my poems, offered invaluable encouragement wrapped up in dry suggestions. I'd met his wife Isabel a few times, his son Ewen once. Not an intimate friendship, then. But for some reason he mattered a great deal to me, still does . . .

I stop. We look at each other. The house is silent, nothing stirring.

'Norman fished a lot of lochs in Assynt,' MacAskill concedes. 'In fact, probably more than anyone else. The Loch of the Green Corrie . . . He said that? His favourite place?'

'Yes.'

'We used to go there with AK MacLeod.'

'He told me. The three of you.'

'Yes. Many times.' He is looking away now, at things not in that room. I wish I could glimpse what he is seeing. We all have our secret store, the one that dies with us.

The silence stretches. This time I resolve to keep my mouth shut. Eventually he looks up. 'I miss him.'

'I miss him too.'

We sit there, finally linked by two true things said. He fumbles in his breast pocket, producing a pencil stub then heavy spectacles.

'I shall require a map . . .'

'I've got one,' I say eagerly.

I stand beside him and open up the map. He peers, the pencil hesitates. He takes off his glasses and peers closer. (That's been happening to me lately – print gets smaller and lighting poorer.) His thick, time-battered finger prods the map, his lips move as he murmurs place names. Come on, come on!

And finally he nods and the pencil descends, underlines. 'Here.'

Yes!

He spends some time pencilling in the route to get there – apparently it is awkward, tricky to find, a steep climb. His parting words are 'We used flies size ten to twelve, mostly Black Pennel and Zulus. And if the wind's from the east, it's no use.'

But I scarcely listen, my head light with relief as I fold the map. He doesn't offer to shake hands, just nods goodbye.

'You'll get permits at the Inchnadamph Hotel. I will hear how you got on.'

He seems confident of that. The parish of Assynt is that sort of place. You catch a fish in a remote loch and the news ripples out. He turns and shuffles indoors. I turn and cross the road to Andy and Peter, map in one hand, thumb up with the other.

'Permits?' Andy says. 'Is that in the spirit of this ploy?'

'I know – but MacAskill seemed definite about it, so maybe we should.'

Peter's doing the map reading, and directs us to the Inchnadamph Hotel as we grumble. It's not the money, more the principle. The history of the Scottish Highlands doesn't make for deep respect of land ownership. There is no Gaelic word for poaching.

On the other hand, fishing fees are part of the income of these estates, which aren't overflowing with money or employment.

Tricky one.

At the head of the long ragged blaze of Loch Assynt lies Inchnadamph. Along with a few scattered houses, it has a phone box, a parking place with picnic table, and a mountain rescue post (unmanned). Like many Highland hamlets, the name is far lovelier than the place. Still, up here any human habitation is noteworthy. For all its beauty, this landscape is the product of a social and environmental disaster.

Over the river and here it is, the Inchnadamph Hotel. Up a drive, with trees around, long and low with a general impression of faded glories. It also seems deeply asleep or simply dead.

Inside is silence, faded tartan carpet, glassy-eyed fish in cabinets. No one at Reception or in the bar. Either everyone is away fishing, or the tide has finally gone out on the Inchnadamph Hotel.

A sullen flat-faced young man appears from the back. What do we want? The surprise is he isn't Australian. Dutch, we reckon, or maybe Austrian. We make the mistake of mentioning the Loch of the Green Corrie. He's suspicious, hasn't heard of it. We show him on the map, he shakes his head. No fishing anywhere without a permit. The hotel has fishing rights. The man who does the permits is not here. Fill in form, please.

Absolutely no eye contact, something between rudeness

and obstructive indifference. The phone rings, he goes away and doesn't return. We look at the form. Name, address. Nationality, car registration. Intended lochs. Fee. Tick the boxes, fill in the form, pay to fish in a small, unvisited, remote loch.

We look at each other.

'Sod this.'

With silent apologies to Mr MacAskill, we hurry out to the car and drive on. The waters of the Loch of the Green Corrie, unlike Blake's Thames, shall remain unchartered.

We head back to Loch Assynt then turn north on the road to Kylesku ('*narrow crossing*'). There are lots of Kyles in the Western Highlands: Kyle of Lochalsh, Kylestrome, Kyles of Bute, Kylerea . . . The crossing at Kylesku is so narrow there's now a bridge across it. I remember waiting there by my father for the tiny two-car ferry to take us across to another world. Bridges are efficient, but few stir a child's heart.

We're into wildness now. Melodramatic presences loom on either side of the empty road through the glen. I stop and we lean over the map. To our left looms the colossal shoulder of Quinag. The shoulder emerges onto a divided summit ridge, both aerial walkways with rock and scree plunging down on either side.

On the right rise the rough scree slopes of Glas Bheinn, 'Green Hill', though it's scarcely that. Gaelic colour words are context-nuanced, sometimes downright misleading. And according to our map, on the far side of Glas Bheinn's summit, high in the throat-hollow of the mountain, is the place where Norman MacAskill's pencil descended and circled: Lochan a Choire Ghuirm. The Loch of the Green Corrie.

After a brief discussion and some map-checking, I finally park the car in a lay-by opposite Loch na Gainmhich, 'Sandy Loch'. A broad spread of glitters, blue at one end, grey beneath cloud at the other, but no sign of sand.

'There'll be fish in there,' Andy says confidently.

Peter wets his finger, holds it in the air.

'What did MacAskill say about the wind from the east?'

Soon we've unwieldy packs loaded on our backs – tents, stoves, mats and sleeping bags, no matter how modern, are bulky. I'm holding my tent under one arm, rod and carrier bags of food in the other hand. Andy and Peter have much the same. The bottles are heavy and clink, the rods are cumbersome. With these loads and the time of day, it's clear we're not going to be carrying this lot up to the Green Corrie, not today at least.

'Base camp at that loch?'

'The shingle beach on the far side.'

Decision made, we leave the car behind and plod off slowly into the promised land, my ski pole standing in for a biblical staff.

Retrieve: ways we get here from there

After stumbling through heather and ditches, we meet the path marked on the map. It is narrow, stony, uneven, not much used. It's good to feel air cool over sweating arms, and walk off the stiffness from today's drive. The path rises, dips, twists then descends towards the east end of Loch na Gainmhich.

Andy's up in front, I hike along with Peter. He talks about a summer Assynt trip with Andy, how they camped below Cul Mor, caught loads of fish and swam and read books, then fished some more.

'I hope this trip is going to be worth your while,' I say. 'I got the impression from the Normans the Green Corrie isn't an easy loch to fish.'

Peter stops, leans his pack back on a boulder.

'When I was doing Aid work in Bolivia, one of the few books I had was MacCaig's *Selected Poems*. I was ill with dysentery, far from home and anyone who spoke well my own language. That book came to mean so much to me.'

I too have stopped and propped my burden on a rock. We're in no hurry. This trip is a chance to get to know friends better.

'Was it hard to settle after South America?'

He looks away at Quinag across the glen, then back at me.

"There comes a point when it's a matter of who you decide to be.'

Andy is calling from the far side of the loch, waving his arms. *Who you decide to be* still resonates in me as we shoulder our burdens. Words written by one man in Edinburgh in the time it takes to smoke a cigarette can reach another lying ill in a village in Bolivia thirty years later, to keep him company and help him know who and where he needs to be.

Andy is already putting up his tent. There's no discussion because this is clearly the place to set up camp. We're on a small rise above the only bit of shingle beach this side of Loch na Gainmhich. The ground is knobbly grass, moss and heather but reasonably dry and not stony, and there's just enough room for three tents.

Open the tent bag, slide out the poles, tent, flysheet. This was my home on the Lhotse Shar trip, my last one with Mal Duff. Fourteen years ago, and still it smells faintly of juniper, smoke, sweat and yak dung.

We each put up our own tent, making home and shelter. This was always one of the defining moments on the Himalayan trips, as notable as crossing the bergschrund, the crevasse that commonly marks the beginning of the mountain proper. Setting up camp is arriving in an empty theatre, marking out the ground where the show will go on. Climbers, fishers – we are players and sole audience, such is the pure nature of the ploy.

A bit like writing poetry, I reflect while skewering the guy ropes into the mossy ground. I mean, the absence of audience. The tiny readership, the impossibility of 'going commercial', guarantees it is written for its own sake. We trust poetry because it's not trying to sell us anything.

Then again, the smallness of the poetry world, the paucity of glittering prizes, seem to generate extraordinary bitchiness, resentment, even malice. *Much hatred, little room* as Yeats wrote about Ireland. Still, it's really not my problem. I write what I want, mostly prose; it has a readership and I make a living. Poetry happens when it happens, and when it does I drop everything else. The work will last or it won't. Meanwhile, there are other cherishable things in life. I have always agreed with MacCaig on that.

I unzip the flap, toss in the karrimat then the sleeping bag and crawl in after them.

It's an orange world in here, quiet and circumscribed, reassuring. I sit cross-legged, taking it in: the smell, the feel of it, these scraps of foreign grass and grit in the corner. This was my home for six weeks below Lhotse Shar, on my last big trip with Mal. He is not here. The person I was then must be around somewhere, though he's a bit of a myth to me.

'Hey Greigy, did you bring your stove along?'

I crawl out. Peter is crouched over a blackened, twisted assembly. It looks like a giant scorched spider.

'It's back in the car. Andy said we wouldn't need it.'

'Right,' Peter says. 'This cup of tea might take some time.'

'Fine,' Andy says casually. 'I'll just do a spot of fishing.'

'No, you'll find some wire to clear this nozzle.'

For a while we are busy making nowhere into somewhere.

Cast: a quick thrash before tea

'I think that's working now,' Peter says, carefully balancing the battered blackened billy on the stove. 'I might just have a quick thrash before tea – call me when it's ready.'

Andy looks startled, then alert. He hurries to his pack and starts unwrapping his rod. A few yards away, Peter is already doing the same. Rods assembled, reels clipped in, lines pulled through, casts tied on: the Dorward brothers in competitive mode. It's a joke of sorts. It's also, I reckon, quite real. It's what they do. I sit and watch and make a few notes of the journey so far. That's what I do. The only fishing that matters to me on this trip lies in the hills behind our camp.

Peter stalks along the shore to my left, scans the loch then works his line out with four lazy, easy swishes. On the fifth pass his line runs out full length, drops lightly. Three flies kiss the still water, three shining rings expand as the cast sinks. His retrieve of the line is a series of gentle, irregular tugs. Then the elbow flexes, the line curls back behind his head; arm comes forward, line streams out, straightens, drops lightly, printing three new circles over the loch.

Yes, he's very good. Reminds me of Mal Duff's casting, maybe even more effortless.

I turn and watch Andy away to my right, standing on a small boulder. I always think of him as the jolly, easygoing one, and Peter a shade more intense. But Andy's whole body-language now is tense and charged. He casts well and skilfully but I can feel the effort going into it. He looks like he's trying; Peter is just doing it.

I think of Norman MacCaig sitting down at his writing table in Edinburgh with a cigarette, casting a line out over his mind and waiting to see what arises.

Along the shore from me, silhouetted against the fierce sunset light to the west, Andy curses quietly. He flexes his rod once more then stops, his line thick with tangle. The secret is to stop casting the moment there's a problem; the natural reaction is to flick the rod again in the hope the line will unsnag. This never works.

As Andy sighs, lays down his rod and sits to address the problem, I give the lamb stew a last stir then go and stand beside him.

'Got a fankle?'

'A bourach,' he says grimly, and takes out his knife.

Further round the loch, Peter retrieves, sends his near-invisible line out to drop three lures lightly on the broken water. He can see what has happened; it will give him a clear ten or fifteen minutes' fishing while his brother sorts this out. He is not actually gloating, just amused.

'A right bourach,' Andy mutters, still struggling to untangle his nylon cast from the thicker floating line. He tells me his father David, a keen etymologist and author of books on Scottish place and family names, gave him the word. A 'fankle' is a tangle that has a chance, with patience and persistence, of being sorted. A 'bourach', pronounced with those tones of gloomy resignation that come so naturally to the Scot, is irreversible. Nothing to be done but cut free the flies, remove the ruined cast and tie on a new one.

As Peter leisurely quarters the water, working the area, Andy snicks the flies off the doomed cast, lays them on his knee. Two Blue Zulus, one Black Pennel. They do not look like any insect I have ever seen. Perhaps trout vision is poor? Yet it is evident they are extremely fussy: wrong fly, no fish.

Maybe fishing flies are not imitations of life-forms so much as metaphors, or far-fetched, appealing similes for what they are not. A hint, a vivid reminder, something to stir the jaded palate of trout or men. Poetry in general, and MacCaig's in particular, does this a lot: a bird fires notes from its soft pea-shooter, a toad looks like a purse, a wild rose bush is a tattered pirate with a bright parrot on its shoulder, a clear night sky is a millstone scattering grains of frost, a deer splashes antlers of water.

Which of course is not true. Simile and metaphor are creative lies, lures to catch the mind's fish by. MacCaig's sensibility was agile with them, and his intellect was often infuriated by this very talent. He constantly reminds us and himself that the natural world is what it is, not like something else nor a metaphor for anything. Even to name the frog, the collie dog, the rose bush, is to lose it.

And yet. And yet it is what we do. And this figurative language restores the world to us. The rose bush is not a pirate, and Quinag across the way is not a 'huddle of anvils', but my God we smile inwardly and picture them anew. Norman repeated this trick, this re-freshing of vision and feeling, all over this landscape, laying out his bright, improbable lures. Now being in Assynt is like fishing inside his head.

A low cry comes downwind from Peter. His rod flicks back once, twice, then his shoulders drop. 'Bigger one,' he calls. 'Lost it.' He casts again, the grey line curls out behind him, flows forward.

Andy works faster. As he ties on the tail fly to the new cast, I wonder: when our lives become tangled, how will we recognise what we can sort out and what we should abandon?

'Right,' Andy says. 'There are fish down the far end, and I'm going to catch them.' He sets off along the shore, ever optimistic, confident he knows fankle from bourach.

Retrieve: what is it necessary to know about Norman MacCaig?

First, that wasn't quite his name. His family name was McCaig. 'MacCaig' was suggested to him early on as his writing name by a Gaelic friend, small-press printer and publisher Callum Macdonald.

The shift is tiny, but illuminating. As with his friends Christopher Grieve (Hugh MacDiarmid) and Robert Garioch (R.G. Sutherland) it helped mark a distinction between the private person and the public writer, or perhaps the public person and the private writer. And Norman MacCaig was very private and very public.

It marks more than that. His mother was a Gaelic-speaker from Scalpay, a small island off Harris in the Outer Hebrides. Though his father, a chemist, was a Lowland Scot, his parents in turn were from Argyll. I sense that the extra letter was a nod, a homage towards that background in the *Gaeltachd*, the Gaelic world. Though Norman was born in Edinburgh in 1910, lived and worked there all his life till he died there in January 1996, and wrote entirely in English, he tended to identify his particular aesthetic disposition with Gaeldom.

Even in later life, his mother's English remained idiosyncratic – in particular, her way of expressing herself in images, unexpected and slightly off-kilter. He believed this had entered into him. In conversation, MacCaig was every bit the Classicist – he got a First in Greek and Latin from Edinburgh University – precise, wry, articulate, controlled. His poetry is transformative, imaginative, at once entranced, formal, playful and straightforward.

His own vision of Gaelic culture, of the Gaelic mind, was resolutely anti-Romantic. He emphasised the love of complex form in Gaelic carving, literature and music. Celtic art could be emotional, particularly the song, but it was emotion mediated through formal control and complexity. In Scottish music, he loved pibroch, the extended high art form of piping. It combines extreme formality, even austerity – this is an instrument that does not permit variation of volume or tone or key, devoid of pauses or inflection – with the intricate patterning of rapid grace notes.

Only late in his life did he casually mention to me he used to play the fiddle. 'Not like Aly [Bain], but quite well.' He also played the chanter, though never the pipes. Apparently he pioneered a mode of fiddle-playing that took pipe tunes and made an equivalent of the grace notes of pibroch.

I am not being over-familiar when I refer to him as 'Norman'. Almost anyone who met him or cared about his poetry does the same. (Revered he might have been, but no one bar intimates referred to MacDiarmid as 'Chris'.) The familiarity speaks of a sense of deep, affectionate connection, of belonging. For Norman MacCaig was not just a poet of the first order. He became for many that much rarer thing: a cherished part of his culture.

*

Norman wrote a very large number of poems, most of them 'in the time it takes to smoke one or maybe two fags'. Not many place-specific ones are set in Edinburgh. Far more concern Scalpay, the Highlands and, above all, Assynt: people, places, lochs, rivers, dogs, birds, frogs, fish. It was his heartland, the core of his inner life. On that last night I spent at his flat, there was such pleasure, longing and loss in his voice when we talked about Achmelvich and the Kirkaig river, AK MacLeod, 'Pollochan', Suilven and Charlie Ross.

He married Isabel Munro, an outstandingly bright and quiet English student at the university. They met at a dance. She was a wonderful dancer and so, he said with pride, was he. Despite his degree, he couldn't get a post as a Classics teacher, and finally opted for primary teaching, which he did for most of his working life. He said he enjoyed it, for he liked people of any age, but when the bell went he walked away from it. 'I'm a teacher,' he would say. 'An easygoing, happy fellow.' So he was, in part.

As a boy he had been disgusted by the images in the illustrated magazines he had read about the Great War; when the Second World War came he knew himself to be a convinced pacifist. He refused to fight and kill, or to aid the killing in any way. His stubbornness and refusal to compromise led from a brief stay in the guardhouse at Edinburgh Castle, to the Non-Combatant Corp, to a spell in Winchester Prison and Wormwood Scrubs. Released, he found work as a jobbing gardener. He neither complained about his treatment nor apologised for his stand. He combined an extreme sensitivity to pain, particularly other people's, with a strong reticence and an absolute obduracy.

After the War, he went back to primary teaching. Now with two small children, Joan and Ewen, they began spending school summer holidays at Achmelvich, three miles from Lochinver, where they rented, at first, a small, dark, basic cottage that faced away from one of the world's loveliest bays. For the next twenty-odd years they spent all the school summer holidays at Achmelvich; after that they rented at Inverkirkaig, up the hill from AK MacLeod's cottage by the bay. The MacCaigs were summer visitors whose attendance was so long-lived, whose love, admiration and engagement were so evident, they became part of the social landscape of Assynt.

He referred to himself as 'an Edinburgh schoolteacher who sometimes writes poetry' rather than a poet. Though he had his pride and his vanities, Norman was very anti-grand. The idea of 'being a poet', as though that were a different and higher form of life, was abhorrent to him. I am with him on this.

He took poetry seriously but he resisted being solemn about it. He was very clear that, rather than being a priestly calling, writing poetry was only one of a number of things he enjoyed. He valued music, reading, fishing and, perhaps above all, whisky and conversation. Many poets are shy, some reclusive or socially unadept. MacCaig bloomed in company. I see him still, standing erect in the blue haze of a pub, surrounded by laughter, argument and anecdote, that great head held high, fag in one hand, glass in the other, listening with his lizard mouth pursed, about to pounce.

The most succinct psychological profile of MacCaig / McCaig I have met was offered by Norman Kreitman, formerly a distinguished psychology research scientist. A lover of poetry as much as of cognitive science, who saw metaphor as being central to both disciplines, he fished with Norman a number of times in the Lothians, as well as meeting him often in public. An old man now, smoking a pipe in his sitting room, he offered me this assessment: *Norman MacCaig was an introvert who became socially expansive in company he found congenial, or was persuaded to view as such through the influence of alcohol.*

I think Norman would have relished that precision.

He was, I think, an observer and a responder, rather than an initiator. He loved to host — his Leamington Terrace flat became the post-pub venue of the postwar Scottish writers, its hospitality unlimited by the hour of night — but not to lead. The true master of the writers' revels at Milne's Bar, the Oxford and the Abbotsford, was the anarchic, exuberant, flamboyant Sidney Goodsir Smith — who died at sixty from alcohol, which had dissolved much of his extraordinary talent. Whereas MacCaig made his interjections, his memorable put-downs, witticisms and retorts, and was able to stand back far enough from his own enthusiasm for whisky to live well into his eighties, writing to the end.

His poetry, like himself, was a balancing act between clear eye, exuberant imagination, a carefully masked childlike heart, and a stringent, sceptical mind. All of these were pronounced in him. The urbanity, wit and intellect were most evident in Edinburgh company. The warmth, the heart, the emotion are most visible in the poetry and in his life in Assynt.

When he writes *I love you, little frog*, or how at AK's funeral *The sea was boring, as grief is/ but beautiful, as grief is not*, the voice is matter-of-fact. It means exactly what it says. My friend Ron Butlin once wrote of Mozart's music 'He is very clear water/ that seems only a few inches deep,/ and yet you will never, never/ touch the bottom.' That touches on MacCaig's art, so apparently simple, so nuanced and profound. He dared to employ words like *lonely, love, marvellous, angry, cruelty, beautiful*. For a major twentieth-century poet — and for me he is that — to use such words unironically is brave, stubborn, and downright radical.

But not sentimental. He intensely disliked displays of feeling, particularly in art. 'If you write with your intellect in charge, put it in an essay. If emotion is in charge, have your hysterics in another room.' That was how he saw poetry, a balancing act between thought and emotion, form and naturalness.

His best work is the kind of poetry that could give poetry a good name. It requires no specialist knowledge, makes no abstruse references. Even the Classical references are deliberately commonplace: Hercules, Alexander, Pythagoras, Socrates, Plato. It doesn't have to be decoded. Starting from the utter obscurity (and formal complexity) of his early, disowned 'New Apocalypse' volumes, he began that 'long haul towards lucidity'.

At first strictly rhymed and metrical, his poems gradually free up. The middle period employs dazzling, casual sleights of off-rhyme and enjambement. The formal qualities are there, to be enjoyed, but not dominating. The later poems are nearly entirely in free verse, of irregular line length, with no clear stanza form. They have sound quality and cadence, but little evident rhyme. The formal capital marking each new line disappears. These poems are bound together by voice alone.

In Scotland, MacCaig's poetry became as widely read and popular as it's possible for poetry to be. After his retirement he did innumerable readings in schools, libraries, festivals, community centres, so many that it seems an entire generation heard him at one time or another. MacDiarmid was revered, Garioch was enjoyed, Crichton Smith highly regarded, George Mackay Brown well known – but of that remarkable generation, probably only Edwin Morgan also became beloved.

Yet MacCaig's reputation scarcely extends across the Border. Outside Scotland I meet good poets, well-read poets, who have barely heard of him. The few who have read him tend to shrug, slightly dismissively. Even in Scotland he is now somewhat overshadowed.

Why is that?

He left behind over a thousand poems and binned many more. The best forty or so are stone-cold winners. That's a lot for any poet. He was open about how quickly and easily they were written. They did not involve months of blood, sweat and tears and multiple drafts, to coax them into existence. Though often subtle and nuanced, they are seldom 'difficult'. They are not Political. (MacCaig's anti-politics, his stress on the reality and value of individual life, as against abstract ideas and causes, may be his one big political idea.)

They are not freighted with Big Ideas – unless moments encountering life, love, beauty, ugliness, loss and death are big ideas. They do not carry information, philosophy, or complex, abstruse references. As such they are not suited to a canon-building coterie, or to academic decoding, being public and democratic.

He did not edit magazines or anthologies; he did not review, or sit on committees or panels of judges. These are how power-bases, influence and connections are built.

Major public events and social trends are scarcely touched on in his poems, except in the most general way. He knew all too well the horrors of the world, but he did not make rhetoric from them, or put his name to causes. Instead he addressed that impossible balancing act we attempt every day, between acknowledging the frequent awfulness in the world and its inhabitants, while responding to the pleasures and wonders we walk through daily, the warmth and friendliness we encounter (particularly, he believed, in Assynt, and I wouldn't disagree). *Noticing you can do nothing about. / It's the balancing that shakes my mind.*

His poems often focus on animals, fish, birds, plants and

lochs, and sometimes people, mostly specific to a small, remote corner of the far North West of Scotland. They appear to be happy, they appear to be 'Nature poems', while being as problematic and subversive as they are memorable, direct and luminous.

His poems are usually short, often playful, and make fun of themselves and their author. All the above tend to tell against his poetry being as highly rated as it merits. Yet I am not alone in finding his best poems shine in the mind like fireflies in the night.

And Norman? At his eighty-fifth birthday celebration at the Queens Hall in Edinburgh he finally, reluctantly, stiffly, got up from his seat in the front row, turned round and looked at us. We rose to our feet, a spontaneous outpouring of affection and regard. He let the applause go on for twenty seconds or so, then raised his hand.

'Stop it,' he commanded. 'You're embarrassing me.'

Laughter, then he sat down. More applause. He loved it. Of course he did. To his mind, there were greater poets, but he knew his worth.

Seamus Heaney, a warm friend and admirer of the man and his poetry, said with appropriate simplicity *He means poetry to me.*

Cast: whisky and conversation

Peter's stove is a battered, sickly, smelly little beast but it has been on all the brothers' annual masochistic camping expeditions, so we have to have it. At times it exudes as much fumes as heat. Crucially, it lacks a simmer control, so at intervals one of us has to reach over and remove one old pan from the heat just before it boils over, swap it for the other blackened pan with the potatoes.

The lamb stew – great chunks of meat bought in Lochinver, onions and garlic, carrots, dried peas, fistfuls of thyme – is starting to look and smell convincing. Peter is a fine and fearless cook and it should work. Out in this heathery wilderness, any food at all seems a miracle. But it's going to be hours till it's ready and I'm starving.

'Oatcakes.'

Andy nods. 'Cheese. *Lots* of cheese.'

'Whisky time?' Peter enquires.

'Definitely.'

I lean back, reach into my pack.

'MacCaig's favourite. And remember it's Glenmorangie as in *orangey*.'

Crack–click of the metal cap as the seal breaks, then the smell rises pungent yet light, dry but slightly sweet, with a hint of salt and sea-pinks. As Andy hacks his penknife into strong Cheddar, and Peter opens the oatcakes, I slosh drams into our mugs and pass them round.

We don't drink this whisky to get drunk. Drunkenness is not the point, the whisky is. Whisky and conversation, two of Norman MacCaig's great loves.

Up till now we've been busy: getting here, putting up tents, laying out the rods and gear; karrimats and sleeping bags unrolled; bacon and milk stored in the loch; coaxing the stove into life. Then Peter and Andy hurried off for exploratory fishing before and after tea, while I sat and watched them and the evening light, made a few notes. The trout score: seven to three in Peter's favour. All small ones, returned to the loch.

Now the rods are carefully propped by the tents and it seems we've fully arrived. We sit around the hissing stove, on the little rise above the shingle beach, as the evening sun lowers a quivering drawbridge across the loch to our camp.

'To the Loch of the Green Corrie.'

'To Norman.'

'To absent friends.'

It seems my palate has been returned to me reconditioned, for this is like drinking the landscape itself, a distillation of water, air and peat.

We sit in silence a while, looking out over the loch into the bulging sun. The breeze fails and a million glitters smooth to one broad blaze. (That last line is MacCaig, 'Tea break by Loch Assynt'. I didn't try to memorise it, but it stuck as things you love do. It's what poets do, become part of our seeing.)

'I don't want these days to pass quickly,' Peter says. His words go out over the water, leaving us with the knowledge they must and will.

Retrieve: one rich day

As we wait for our stew, it is story time.

From the mid-Sixties the *Weekend Scotsman* printed new poems in a discreet boxed-off corner. Though as a teenager my inner life was mostly informed by music, those unsung lines interested and moved me. Unlike the songs of Dylan, Leonard Cohen, Ray Davies, these words referenced my country. Certain names kept appearing; Iain Crichton Smith, George Mackay Brown, Norman MacCaig, Edwin Morgan.

One weekend I cut out a group of four short MacCaig poems, including 'Tea break by Loch Assynt' and 'Rich day', which mentioned Canisp. I knew Loch Assynt, I'd climbed Canisp one long day with my father. In 'So many summers', I knew the abandoned boat pulled up on the grass and the hind's delicate skeleton, though I had never seen them. Now I had. That's how the words worked, they implanted images, and they could be summoned any time just by murmuring the words anew.

I have that cutting still, I tell Peter and Andy. Our budgie got to it, and nibbled serrations all round the outside, then pecked a few holes in the accompanying photo of the poet, his long, handsome, melancholy face hiding a grin, cigarette in his right hand. For many years it lay under the glass top of my little desk where I scrawled and typed, a talisman and a reminder of what I wanted for myself: a poem in the *Weekend Scotsman*.

Some thirty years later I was with Norman in the Auld Toll Bar in Bruntsfield. We were sitting alone in one of its little booths. It would be the last time I had a drink out with him. He'd announced he would need to take a taxi back – his legs, circulation problems. He did not mention the heart attacks I found out about only recently, from his son Ewen.

'The doctors keep telling me to give up these.' He waved the cigarette, the little baton that conducted all his remarks. He admitted he had once stopped smoking. ('Yes, that was after his first heart attack,' Ewen said. 'He smoked forty a day on non-drinking days, and more when there was a dram.') Said he hadn't found it too hard, but in that time he wrote no poems. Nothing. Not a metrical sausage. Not even a free verse one, the kind without rhymes, the tricky kind. Then one day he went down to the corner shop, bought a packet of cigarettes, sat down and smoked while writing three new poems.

'Two of them were quite good, and I have never stopped smoking since. Now I buy Silk Cut, which is an expensive way of smoking fresh air.'

He had a way of swivelling his eyes in one's direction and then away again, as if he was rolling a thought like a bright marble around inside his head.

'Have I told you that story before?'

'Yes, Norman.'

He giggled, that little hissing laugh. I saw in him the old man and the mischievous boy, the wit and the man whose wife and old friends had gone.

Maybe that was why I told him about his poems I'd cut out of *The Scotsman*, and how he was partly responsible for my committing to poetry. I said I had never forgotten one of them, 'Rich day', ever since I had read it in the late Sixties.

That eye-swivel again.

'I don't think I know that one. How does it go?'

Old he might be, but Norman never lost his nose for potential bullshit. I drank from my pint, calling up that budgie-nibbled clipping, the words, the lay-out. Then I recited it back to him, quietly amid the busy bar, into his better ear.

When I finished, he was silent, thoughtful. Then he beamed.

'That's quite good. I like that!'

I am glad I had the opportunity to speak back a poem to its maker towards the end of his life, to demonstrate how these things ripple out, endure when so much else does not. The desk at the window in the flat where he wrote it is gone, as is the man, as is the day he wrote about, spent fishing with friends in a lochan below Canisp. But the poem remains in my head, though it is not in any of his collections or the *Collected Poems*. Perhaps I am the last person who knows it.

I end my pre-prandial story with the poem, that Andy and Peter and you might remember it. As we sit on the heathery knoll in the lowering sun and drink Glenmorangie, I recite the lines and feel layer upon layer of memory, MacCaig's and mine, fold and fall upon each other like small waves onto the shore of Loch Na Gainmhich.

Rich day

All day we fished
the loch clasped in the throat
of Canisp, that scrawny mountain,
and caught trout and
invisible treasures.

We walked home, ragged millionaires,
our minds jingling, our fingers
rustling the air.

And now, lying on the warm sand,
we see
the rim of the full moon
rest on a formal corrugation of water
at the feet of
a Britannia cloud:
sea and sky, one golden sovereign
that will never be spent.

Norman MacCaig

Cast: overboard on the thyme

As he crouches over his little stove that sprawls beneath the pan, the low sunlight off the loch emphasises the lines curved down Peter's cheeks. Also those around his eyes and across his forehead.

We first met when he was seventeen. Andy introduced him as 'Ned, my schoolboy brother'. He snorted but shook hands with me before elbowing his older brother in the ribs. The 'Ned' was on account of his being a tearaway with girls and the local youths. Like all Andy's friends I called him Ned for years, until he came back from his two years doing medical Aid work in Nicaragua and Bolivia. At that point I realised he didn't actually like being called that, and anyway he was getting too old to be a boy racer.

Peter tastes, frowns, shreds some more wild thyme into the stew and stirs again. He's the foodie, and a good cook of vivid Spanish seafood and tapas. I have never eaten a meal cooked by Andy.

Certainly you would know them brothers. Voices, cadences, features, temperaments – they are not the same but they as it were rhyme. Some elements full rhyme (their eyes, ears, foreheads, for instance), some half-rhyme (chins, skin tone), some distantly rhyme (hairline, build, outlooks).

Peter speaks South American Spanish with relish and a lot of guttural throat-clearing. Andy has fluent High German, enjoys doing business and socialising in that language. Andy and Andrea are married. Peter and Deborah are not – she in particular has no intention of being. 'Hangover from my intense feminist period,' she says and laughs, unapologetically. They have two children, Jack and Jamie, so pale and fair they seem like images over-exposed to light.

Yes, divergences. I glance over at Andy, who sits cross-legged in front of his tent, mug of whisky in one hand, book of John Buchan's *Montrose* in the other. He chuckles, turns the page, sips.

'My brother has a tranquil inner soul, he's comfortable in his own skin,' Peter remarked on the path today. Though both share a default enthusiasm, energy and openness, Andy is almost unfailingly positive and sunny. His work is demanding and stressful, but that seldom seems to stress him. Andy is energetic; Peter is restless. Andy is *Can do*; Peter is *Why?*

As he reads, glances up at the loch then back at the page, Andy Dorward seems untroubled and completely at ease. He was once, briefly, very ill; that apart, in the first forty years of his life, nothing very bad has happened to him. No tragedies, unemployment, divorces, broken hopes or lost ideals.

Being intelligent, informed, open to others, he is well aware of how bad and tough, painful and unfair life can be. But it is his nature to be happily enthusiastic, to take problems and solve the ones that can be solved, and not brood on the ones that cannot. If he has dark nights of the soul, they remain pretty well hidden.

Andy Dorward is a fortunate man. Fortunately he appreciates it, and spreads his positivity, his sense of pleasure and enjoyment of living, his love of good ploys. I may sometimes be mystified at his untroubled nature, but I cannot grudge him it. Any more than, in the end, I envy it.

He looks up from his book. 'How's the very slow stew coming along, Ned?'

Peter replies in Spanish, something to do with patience and sons of dogs. Andy chuckles, sips, goes back to his book. 'Let me know if I can help.'

Peter says something about his *cojones* being beaten on the anvil of Time (I think). He stares into the rich-smelling stew. I notice his dark brown hair, brushed back to show the same slight widow's peak as his brother's black hair, is thinning. Which amuses Andy, because his isn't.

Apparently the family myth was that Peter was 'clever, because I could do Science'. Andy was the imaginative, arty one. Which meant that by default, Peter wasn't. He studied Medicine, largely because he admired a doctor uncle. Uncle Morrison had warmth, gentleness and gravitas that came, Peter felt, from deep experience of human beings. 'I thought if I was a doctor, I might become like that.'

When Peter showed me the novels and stories he had begun to write, I couldn't square their relentlessly pessimistic outlook with the energetic, purposeful, enthusiastic person I thought I knew.

How long it can take to change one's picture of someone, no matter the evidence to the contrary. MacCaig is still thought of as 'easy-oasy and jocose', and his poems essentially upbeat, reassuring, celebratory and undemanding, though little of this is true. Much of this image was fostered by himself. I think now the social man was the mask. I think the poems, with their bright living world gnawed around by darkness until latterly that darkness leaves only a few bright bones gleaming amid the loss and loneliness, I think they are the inner man, the real MacCaig.

Andy puts down his book and looks over the water. 'Must get Jack and Jamie here when they're older,' he says. Andy is devoted to his nephews; one of the few downsides of New York is he doesn't see them enough. He loves being an uncle, taking them round Scottish castles, telling ghost stories, histories. The question of his own childlessness has never been aired.

'Hola, amigos!' Peter cries in his Speedy Gonzales voice. 'Ze food, eet is not yet ready, I theenk!'

We break out more oatcakes and refill the mugs with Glenmorangie cut with loch water, for we'd had to leave our wine in the car. We sit cross-legged round the stove above the loch in the fading sunset glow and wait intently.

Even as we've watched, the light has drained away, depositing layers of saffron on the north-west horizon. Higher up, turquoise lakes brim inside burning shores. Loch na Gainmhich reflects it all back, so faithfully it looks like there is no water at all, just dying light redoubled.

For the first time today, it's a little chilly, and our mood seems to have dipped. Today has been travel, meeting up, discovery. Now we're here, nowhere else.

Andy zips up his fleece.

'Going for a piss,' he says, and wanders off along the uneven shore, hands in pockets, head down.

Peter and I watch him go. Then he glances at me. That assessing doctor's gaze.

'The post-op effects of brain trauma and invasive surgery are long-lasting,' he says quietly. 'What do you feel like now?'

A new slit of light has opened up above the horizon. Below it, a crimson bleeding, then darkening heather and emptiness. Andy is standing on a little headland, staring at the water, at the centre of his world as I am of mine.

What do I feel like?

'Some stronger cheese for a start,' I say. 'I bought a nippy one to go with the whisky. It's behind you.'

Peter grins, lobs over the nippy cheese. I cut it open with my fishing knife, impale us a chunk each. Just because we're each alone the centre of our own world doesn't mean we can't share cheese and conversation.

'God, this is so good!' Peter exclaims.

'Yeah,' I say, and we smile at each other in recognition. 'It is good to be here.'

And once again, it is. We clink mugs, Peter jabs a fork into the potatoes then quickly substitutes the stew pan back onto the blue-yellow flame.

'Hey, guys – saw a really big fish rise out there!' Andy is stumbling back up the little rise to our camp. 'Reckon I'll give it a thrash tomorrow morning first thing, before we go up to the Green Corrie.'

'You'll have to start early to make up a seven-three deficit,' Peter murmurs.

'I'd settle for the biggest fish.' Andy grins at me. 'Peter may sometimes catch more, but I usually get the biggest one.'

'My brother's a romantic,' Peter remarks as he deftly switches the pans. 'Someone who can't distinguish wish from fact. Grub up!'

Andy drags a karrimat from his tent to sit on. We're finally ready to eat. *Nothing stops this*, I think: the bubbling pan, the slow-oncoming dark, the light more lurid as it dies. Our choice is whether to cherish it, mourn its passing, or feel as little as possible.

'Got your plate?'

I hold out my tin plate. Peter dollops up stew then spuds in the gloaming. We're far north and it won't get much dimmer now.

'This is fantastic, Ned!' Andy slurps.

Meat coarse yet soft, gravy rich with wine and herbs, buttery potatoes, bread, mug of whisky – not sophisticated but here by the loch side it's miraculous.

'Thanks, Peter,' I say.

Peter–Ned ducks his head, pleased, acknowledging.

'I maybe went a bit overboard on the thyme,' he says.

But then again, the Glenmorangie murmurs in my head, who does not?

'Sometimes you don't know how starving you are until you get fed,' Andy says, and his words ripple out and fade over the darkening loch and hills of Assynt.

Retrieve: a night out

'What thou lovest well remains, the rest is dross'
– *Cantos*, Ezra Pound

There comes a time to put the notebook aside – how long a day this one has been! – and let be. Alone, without book, radio or music, I lie in my sleeping bag in the not-dark of a northern summer midnight. The fabric expands then sags, night's diaphragm.

There is an elemental satisfaction in sleeping in a tent, or any form of temporary shelter. The tougher the surroundings, the sweeter when you finally crawl inside, zip up the flap, pull off boots and stow them carefully, then start creating order for the night ahead: torch, water-bottle, chocolate, dry socks, pillow of folded clothes.

Twig walls, canvas, Gore-Tex fabric – they are permeable to the world in a way a house is not. At any time of night one may wake to feel breeze passing, smell the night, hear the world going about its darktime business. Trees rattle and creak, water gathers, animals hide, are dispatched in scuffles and squeals, and the self lies wakeful, sheltered and somehow consoled at the heart of it.

A mutter from Peter's tent. The faint glow of his torch goes out as he stops reading *Love in the Time of Cholera*.

We come into a one-man tent as though into ourselves. Sealed off yet permeable, we are human Gore-Tex. Three friends, each in his own tent, each alone in his breathing, each connected. This night lochside is our common ground. Our lovers, friends, family, the dead, are not here, yet they too are with us.

I have no desire to write or to sleep. This calm hour, as much as any fish, is what I came here for. I lie and wait for whatever arises.

On the '86 Lhotse Shar expedition, this worn tent was my home. Weeks of high-altitude sunlight have left its fabric pale and fragile. It still smells faintly of yak dung smoke, jasmine twigs, roll-ups and mountain-sweat. I reach out, dip my hand in the little pocket where I used to store my glasses, notebook, pen and lighter. The grit on my finger-tips must be from Upper Nepal. I sniff, wondering, waiting.

What comes to me is not the days we endured, suffered and laughed on those expeditions. Nothing dramatic or drastic. Now all those revels are long ended and my friend is dead, what returns is a night Malcolm and I passed without shelter, succour or sleeping bags, among the Karakoram mountains of Baltistan.

The Mustagh Tower expedition was over. The big hill had been climbed. John, Sandy and Alex were going on to attempt Broad Peak. That was not part of my remit; I'd had my experience, my story, our diaries. Time to go home, write the book, eat bacon and drink beer and wine, lie in a wide soft bed with my lover. (Home, I would soon discover, is where the problems start. The demands and problems of expeditions are defined, finite and can be resolved; those that come with tax returns and faithless love never are while you breathe.)

At the last moment, Malcolm decided to walk out with me. He had climbed his hill, he was frazzled and missed Liz. Broad Peak wasn't going anywhere and besides it was not very interesting. So one morning we shook hands with our friends, then with light packs and three porters we turned away from the Mustagh Tower, clambered down to the Baltoro glacier, and trudged happily homewards across the undulating, loose moraine.

On that long walk out we replayed and reflected on the expedition, but mostly we talked of home, of food, fishing and future ploys. Mal pretended to be hard-bitten and realistic, but he was a hope-filled romantic whose heart kept slipping down his sleeve.

The long days of trudging were also time to talk of family, childhood, the alcoholic father who had taught him to cast and fish, and my father who had died five weeks before the trip had begun, an event that had not yet had time to catch up with me. Often we walked apart, just thinking and covering ground, then finally just walking, thoughtless and free. Each evening we caught up with the porters, pitched tents, ate and brewed and turned in. Each day brought us lower, into more oxygen, more energy, bigger appetite and deeper sleep. Fully acclimatised, we skittered cheerfully over the loose moraine we had so toiled up on our way to the mountain.

It must have been the third or fourth day, late afternoon, the glacier left behind. We plodded along like refugees from *The Waste Land*, across red rock, over red dust, through dried-up red ravines. K5 and the Lobsang Spire's huge sundial spike disappeared at our backs. The porters as usual had gone on ahead, wanting to get their day's darg – work – over. Then in that barren place we came to a river that cut right across our trail.

We stood and looked at it. It was fast and tumbling, grit-grey and opaque. We cautiously prodded our poles into the depths. Under the rushing water was a grinding grumbling as stones were swooshed down.

'Glacier melt,' Mal commented. 'We've got here too late in the day.'

We climbed up the ridge, looking for the porters. No movement anywhere. They had our tents, stoves, food, clothes and sleeping bags.

We looked at each other, then back at the river. It was ferocious, unstable, ice-cold. A slip there could be very bad. Then again we were getting hungry and the sun was turning red as it birled towards the horizon.

Twice we started on the crossing, twice we turned back.

'I'm not coming all this way to get injured here,' Mal said at last. 'And I promised Kath I'd get you back in one piece. It should be do-able in the morning. Okay?'

I looked at the melt river, then at the bare ground all around us.

'Okay.'

There wasn't much there. A boulder, a scraggy wild rose in that empty, mountain-locked valley. We checked our supplies: a chocolate bar, some K2 cigarettes. We had our karrimats strapped to our packs, camera, suncream, notebook, shades, sunhat, inner gloves. We had only half a litre of good water – the grit-filled meltwater was not drinkable, our doctor had warned us of gall stones.

The sun went down without drama. No clouds, so no conflagration in the west. The sky became very clear, a thin, stretched blue. We zipped up our fleeces, unrolled the mats behind the big rock then sat and waited as night came silting up the valley.

In the near-dark we finished the chocolate for our supper, sipped the water, had a cigarette each, harsh and sweet. We talked for a while, recalling the Edinburgh buses and the guff of the breweries. It seemed very distant and dear to us. Finally Mal positioned his rucksack and lay down with it under his head. Hands in pockets for warmth, I lay down on my mat and waited.

Long silence, watching the stars register, one by one.

'I hope we don't have to cuddle each other for warmth.'

'Christ, so do I.'

Pause.

'We'll cross in the morning.'

'Yes.'

'Goodnight, dude.'

'Night.'

We lay there, stretched out on our backs like figures on an Arundel tomb, without the hand-holding and the loyal dog.

The sky was star-studded and deep. The stars do not twinkle at altitude; there are so many one cannot recognise familiar constellations. They are just there, fixed, unfaltering.

So many many stars. I never felt so boundaryless as under that Karakoram night sky. I looked back up at the stars and then it began to happen, that shift I was to remember fourteen years later in a tent in Assynt, and retrieve now in my writing shed in suburban Edinburgh.

Abruptly, the stars were *down there*. I was looking down on them from a vast height. I felt giddy, looking down into that vertiginous drop. At any moment I would fall off the Earth, into space. I spread my hands on the ground, but there was nothing to grip there. Nothing to hold on to anywhere. Nothing to do but wait to be sucked down and out, nothing for it but to fall.

I lay, awe-struck and helpless, until I had to surrender, and I fell into the night.

When Buddhist friends talk of the Void, so magnificent and awful to look into, I always picture it studded with stars.

There is only so much expansion one can take. We go into our dying with a handful of memories, as an explorer might take a knife, a flint, length of cord and a twist of tea into the wildness. MacCaig knew that. Who we truly are is not in our obituaries but in those final items.

What came to me, to keep me through that night? The bend of the stream at Bannockburn, surface darker where it slowed. My grandfather's witty face, flushed in late sun, his trilby hat tipped back, eternal cigarette smoke rising. A girl in a white dress crossing red sand. The albino blackbird pink-eyed at the window of our garden shed; rabbits coming near at hand, under the rhododendrons at dusk.

White dunes at Achmelvich Bay, scent of sea-pinks, coarse marram grasses and bog myrtle.

Memories of the planet we have loved, how we'll need them as we go.

That night passed with some sleep, some wakefulness, some states that cannot be named. Dawn came; we were damp with condensation, cold, hungry and out of cigarettes. We rolled up our mats, drank the last of the water, stretched and went down to the river. It was still glacier-melt grey and opaque, but shrunken now its mountain sources had frozen overnight. Using our poles, we hopped and hurried across, wrung the icy water from our boots ('Okay, matey?') and set off in search of the nearest village and our porters, and whatever breakfast we could find.

A minor cock-up, a small incident, yet it glows still in my mind when all the dramas of the Mustagh Tower expedition have become distant and improbable, as though they happened to someone else. But that night happened to *me*.

In a way it is happening still. It will be one of the last memories of being human I take with me, when I fall into the starry night.

DAY 2

Cast: passing on Iron John

My eyes open onto orange sky a couple of feet up.

No sound from the other tents. I dress, leave my watch behind and crawl out. The loch is ruffled by an easterly wind; the broken sky could go one way or the other. In the heather lies the Glenmorangie bottle, clear and empty as my head.

The oddest thing, we agree, sitting on the shingle with the first brew of the day, is how well we feel. We have a taste for beer, wine and whisky, but lack the stamina of the night-long drinker, or the desire for oblivion of the true drunk. For us a bottle of whisky in one session is a *lot*.

'I think we did some happy haivering last night,' Andy says.

'Haivering, definitely.'

'Someone will have to fetch the other bottle and wine for tonight.'

We look away across the loch and moor to the black dot of my car, our connection back into a world that already seems improbable.

Peter yawns, stretches.

'Going for a dip.'

'Me and all!'

I watch, impressed, approving and entirely unenvious as they go in. It's all a bit Iron John for me. They are very keen and clean, these lads.

The brothers Dorward swim and shout. Out in the loch, a small fish jumps and hangs curved for a moment, like a silver bracket. At the far shore, another fish jumps, closing a wordless parenthesis.

I stir the porridge, add a little more salt, reach for the milk and honey.

Retrieve: a dip in Deep Time

While we wait for the Dorward brothers to finish their morning ablutions, and I sit gazing at Quinag across the way, it is time to get up to speed with some geology.

The hills of Assynt are unique in Scotland. Cul Mor, Cul Beag, Bheinn Mor Coigeach, Suilven, Stac Pollaidh, Canisp, Quinag, Glas Bheinn – each sits out on its own, each with an entirely different profile. They are arranged like trophy heads along the wall of a shooting lodge, with gaps of undulating moor sprinkled with lochans and grey bedrock between each exhibit.

More scientifically, the bedrock of this valley, like much of Assynt, is Lewisian gneiss. It is a metamorphic rock, a rehash of the earliest parts of the Earth's crust, formed as the molten mantle of the planet cooled. It is dense, hard, a pleasing grey colour. When I was young, my father told me it was the oldest rock known on the planet (true at the time). I felt proud it was in my country, and intrigued to be told it was also to be found in eastern parts of North America. At that time Continental Drift was thought to be an improbable, irresponsible theory, lacking both hard evidence and a mechanism of plate tectonics.

So the rock I sit on this morning is about three billion years old. It contains no fossils, because it pre-dates multicellular life on our planet. This stuff under my hand and poking out as boulders in the water where the Dorward boys shout enthusiastically, is *early*. It has completed a near circumnavigation of the globe since its formation.

Sitting on their Lewisian gneiss base, the bulk of these 'pachydermatous mountains' is mixed reddish sandstone. They are the remains of sedimentary layers laid down by vast rivers flowing into the interior of the continent Laurentia, carrying eroded fragments of long-vanished mountains. These sedimentary layers were once some five miles thick – roughly the height of Everest. (I once sat wrapped in my sleeping bag at Advanced Base Camp on our Everest expedition, staring at the moonlit limestone Yellow Band that runs through the mountain at around 27,000 feet, trying to grasp that it contains fossils from the seabed.)

These reddish sandstones date from over a billion years after the Lewisian gneiss they sit on. (To be clear, a billion to geologists is a thousand million.) The Laurentia continent that included Assynt drifted over the Earth's mantle from the South Pole to the Equator. The Jurassic period left partial fossils of dinosaur in Skye, no distance from here.

The drift continued to roughly where North America is now. There the Moine schists to the east of Assynt were added to the Lewisian block. Fragments of micro-continents that included the Southern Uplands, England and Southern Ireland lay to the south across the Iapetus Ocean, somewhat wider than the Atlantic is now. The Iapetus Ocean closed until about 410 million years ago 'Scotland' and 'England' finally met and consolidated along the Iapetus Suture, approximately where Hadrian's Wall is today. Then the newly assembled British Isles split from North America and moved eastward as the Atlantic Ocean opened up.

Around the summit of Quinag, and some of the other Assynt mountains, there is a cap of quartzite. Even at this distance, it's clearly different from the bulk below it. A form of near-pure sedimentary quartz, it was laid down on top of the sandstone a billion years later, at a time when the whole landmass was at the bottom of a vast freshwater lake. And after the quartzite was consolidated, the whole mass was thrust up again.

The ground I sit on this morning has rafted across much of the globe, and this small part of Scotland is probably the most travelled landmass on our planet. It has been under the ocean, been desert, freshwater lake, covered by miles-deep sandstone, then under water again. It has had no life, fishes, dinosaurs then no dinosaurs, thousands of feet of ice. The ice melts, returns, melts again, carves out these extraordinary mountains. We are now in the Holocene Interglacial period, and it is too early to say whether the Ice Age is over, or merely taking a break before returning to make global warming seem a benign temporary blip.

The planet is not stable and never has been. Why should it be? It was not made for us. We are here because of its instability. One day we may not be, for the same reason.

Very, very recently, in the last minute of the Earth's year, early humans appear, retreat from the oncoming ice, return as the last glaciers grind and melt away from here just twelve thousand years ago. They would have looked on something very like this wide valley pared back to the original gneiss, these eroded sandstone mountains, that pale quartzite cap on Quinag, as yet unnamed.

Geologists talk about Deep Time. Considering it seriously has a similar effect to looking at the thousand billion stars of our Milky Way at night and spotting among them the fuzz of the Andromeda galaxy. Deep Space. When I was young, astronomers knew of five galaxies. By 1999, this had increased to 125 billion. The current estimate is of up to 500 billion other galaxies.

The mind stalls. It wasn't made for driving this kind of information.

Much of the time the stars are not visible. But the landscape's geological narrative is available anytime. That's why I've taken the time to learn its basics, so I can inform and blow my mind any time I need perspective.

Deep Space, Deep Time. Contemplating them makes your head birl. Terrifying or strangely relaxing, they make it impossible to take anything very seriously again.

Except, right now, breakfast.

Cast: in search of the Green Corrie

Andy and Peter are dressed, we have shared breakfast of porridge and flapjacks. With a flourish Peter produces a small Italian espresso maker.

'Time for a quick one, amigos?'

Yes, we have time. There is a lot of it about, and the Loch of the Green Corrie is not going anywhere, and the bittersweet kick of coffee is life itself.

With day-packs containing waterproofs – this is the North West Highlands – food, flask, sweater, camera, rods and fishing gear, we head straight up the steepening slope behind our tents, not exactly competing but certainly testing ourselves.

The terrain is rough turf, boulders and heather, with small crags that can be scrambled or turned on either side. Into the slope now, the wind is cut off, the sun fierce. On a steep pull-up, the ground is inches from my face, and I see close-up the fine grit, rabbit droppings, quartzite sparkle, pale new grass between old heather roots. I feel it, I smell it. Feel too my body, the lungs working hard, heart pumping in my neck, the sear of muscle down my calves – everything that says I'm embodied, now, in this place.

A clear, high-pitched *mew-mew*. High in the gully, we stop, look up and watch a solitary buzzard drift across the glare. The black outer wing feathers separate, flick like the fingers of a hand, and the bird silently tilts our way. Riding the up-current, it circles over us. I can see the white bars on the underside of its broad wings, see the grey hooked bill turn from side to side. In the stillness and silence, I sense the heartbeat that powers it, as mine does me. For a moment I glimpse us from its yellow eyes: three two-legged stringy life-forms with pale upturned faces.

Too big to be prey, too earthbound to be a threat, we are not of much interest. The buzzard utters another shrill, dismissive *mew-mew*, flexes its wings stiffly then glides off over the bealach.

Smiles and silent nods bind us together, then Andy turns and clambers on up. I follow him, thinking how rarely I encounter the wild. Household and farm animals do not carry that charge of otherness. But those rabbits I knew in childhood, under the bushes at dusk, so close to I heard them breathe, hiding near them was to dizzily glimpse a life quite other. The small trout that jumped from the water an hour ago, to hang like silvery parentheses across the loch, they came from a different world. That buzzard might as well be sent from the daylight moon that hangs over the shoulder of Glas Bheinn.

Gasping, hearts loud in our ears, we pull over the top and onto the bealach. I call for a tea-break. We sit up there, looking down on our tents far below. Across the way, Quinag slumbers in Deep Time; the quartzite cap that the last glaciers failed to entirely remove is pale against the blue.

The buzzard, a speck moving across the shoulder of Glas Bheinn, drifts in its own micro-seconds.

Meanwhile back in human time we drink tea and gaze out over the scattered sunlit islands beyond Quinag, debating whether they can be the Summer Isles (they are not). Sheffield, London, New York are now fanciful as castles seen in clouds. This sweating body, this slowing heart, the sweet crumbling of biscuit in the mouth, this warm moor-smelling ground that falls and rises all around us are as real as it gets.

There is little we can say of happiness, other than we've been there.

'Wow!' Andy says. 'Look at this.'

He is pointing among the heather. We crawl closer, part the roughness and look down on a tiny frog. 'Here's another!' Peter says. Green and yellowish back, black yellow-rimmed eyes blinking on top of the little wedge-shaped snout. The front feet move cautiously, so thin-skinned they're almost transparent.

I put my hand down carefully and pick one up. A cool-ness on my palm, the size of a halfpenny. The throat gulps. We study each other, then it springs off my hand.

Froglets, the place is crawling with living jewels. We're not sure whether they are heading up towards the tiny lochans, or downhill to the big ones. But we're all thinking the same: MacCaig.

Norman MacCaig's eye and heart were drawn to animals. He was not highly knowledgeable about them; he could name the commonest birds and that was about it. I think he didn't want to know more, believing that knowledge of their Latin names, habitat, feeding and mating patterns, moulting season would obscure their reality. Sometimes the more you know, the less you see. What you encounter is your knowledge, not the thing itself.

So he looked as a poet looks, not as an ornithologist. He looked with wonder at the otherness of sparrow, stonechat, swallow, finch, gannet, buzzard. Being himself, he transformed them through image, simile, metaphor – and then hastily repented, tried to return them to their otherness. The poem then typically reflected on himself, the observer, the transformer, stuck with this eye that noticed, heart that opened, and mind that made everything into something else.

With MacCaig the natural world is endlessly teasing, tantalising, yielding frustrating glimpses into itself and oneself. Wonder, yes, but also strangeness and perplexity. And at the beginning, in that first glimpsing, before all the conjuring, reflection and cleverness, there arises that thin-skinned, quivering capaciousness: love.

We move on up with a renewed sense of connection, watching where our feet fall.

Retrieve: two kinds of frogs

Eight years later Ewen McCaig briskly asserted 'Of course my father's Assynt was all just a fantasy, a projection.' That's been troubling and interesting me for a while now.

On one level it must be true. Just as our bright, improbable fishing flies were not so much imitations of as oblique references to the bug life they stood in for, so the world of poems exists in and for the imagination. It can never be 'the real world', nor is it meant to be.

For those of us who cannot claim to have a definitive handle on reality – who cannot but be aware there are as many takes on it as there are people, and that's before we even start on the animals' version – there is always the world brought home to us by other means. For us, poems, novels, songs, music, oh very well let's say *Art*, is not a pleasant frivolity, a decoration daubed over the 'real world', but as real as it gets. That is, real within our minds.

So there they were that morning, beneath our feet and in our minds: real frogs and MacCaig frogs. The former, already a memory as I write this, now glow alongside the latter. Like the rotting boat and the hind's skeleton in MacCaig's 'So many summers', with every year it is harder to tell the difference between them.

I have great respect for those who precisely observe, detail, categorise the natural world, the ones who are prepared to count the number of bars on a buzzard's wing, who know at a glance a male from a female frog. Such dedication is a kind of love. It aims to know the world through detailing it. It deals in observable fact, mechanisms and testable theory.

There are other ways of knowing the world, such as through the image, the glimpse and the word. Rilke wrote that works of art are of an infinite loneliness, and can be little apprehended by criticism; only love can grasp and hold and fairly judge them. I suggest this also applies to the natural world and the beings in it.

A poem is not a proposition, and it deals not in knowing but in experiencing. It is more akin to an incantation, a shamanistic enactment, a verbal virus.

While prose is divided into fiction and non-fiction ('lies and facts', my father would growl), poetry is neither. Larkin's 'They fuck you up, your mum and dad' is not an observation-based testable psychological theory. It is the poem's rhetoric. Likewise the conclusion 'Get out as early as you can/ And don't have any kids yourself' is not an offering from a government think-tank on population growth.

Sitting at this table in the garden shed eight years on, watching us climb uphill through MacCaig country in search of both the real and the imagined Loch of the Green Corrie, I'm confronting again lies and facts and something that is neither. As on that hillside thighs begin to burn and the air sears at unused parts of our lungs, I'm thinking of the last time I saw Norman MacCaig alive.

It was at the launch of Roderick Watson's *The Poetry of*

Scotland 1380–1980. MacCaig was guest of honour. I was shocked at how much he'd aged since that last night at his flat. He was helped to a chair and sat as though he did not expect to get back up. When he was asked to read, he stayed seated. His introduction was weary, wry, precise, casual and considered. We were, after all, his final audience.

This is what he said, near verbatim.

'When I am dead – which will be quite soon – I shall probably be known as "the frog poet".' (*Pause, laughter*) 'They say I write a lot of poems about frogs.' (*Pause*) 'I do. I like them.' (*Pause*) 'This is a poem about a frog.'

Then he read, the heavy book shaking in his mottled hands.

My last word on frogs

People have said to me, *You seem to like frogs.*
They keep jumping into your poems.

I do. I love the way they sit,
compact as a cat, and as indifferent
to everything but style, like a lady remembering
to keep her knees together. And I love
the elegant way they jump and
the inelegant way they land.
So human.

I feel so close to them
I must be froggish myself.
I look in the mirror expecting to see
a fairytale Prince.

But no. It's just sprawling me,
croaking away
and swivelling my eyes around
for the stealthy heron and his stabbing beak.

Norman MacCaig

Cast: first contact

I see us now as from the buzzard's eye, three multicoloured life-forms labouring up over the folds, gullies and ridges of Glas Bheinn, our shadows short and emphatic in the midday sun. I'm seeing the scene not just from above but from beyond – I mean from now, in this Edinburgh shed, the day outside bright and frozen, rare snow stuck to the laurels and the eucalyptus. Its accuracy is of course uncheckable, but it is what I see, or what the words lead me to see. About that I do not lie to you.

Either we did not have a compass that day, or we were incompetent. In either case, we got lost. The pathless terrain was complex, downright odd, confusing us with its angles, dips, crags and gullies. We came to a tiny lochan, then a larger one. We looked at it, then at the map. It was one of those *If we are here, we should go there* situations. We tried to go there. The ground got steeper till we were scrambling first on loose scree then on rock.

High in the throat of Glas Bheinn, we came on another lochan. Was this it? Though it was gripped in a corrie, it didn't look the right shape. Perhaps this was the Loch of the Red Corrie. We looked down over several scattered lochans. We looked at them, then at the map, trying to connect the two.

'I think we should go on up,' Andy said.

'I think we're too high,' Peter said, studying the contours.

We went up. Sweat dripped down my hair, the pack clung to the back of my shirt. Fleeces were now wrapped round waists, hats stuffed in pockets. It's not masochism that gives me pleasure in effort and physical discomfort, nor is it the joy of stopping, though that was there too. It is the sense of connection with the world the striving body brings.

No one has written about what it is to be in the mountains, in one's body, as well as Nan Shepherd. *The Living Mountain* makes my skin prickle, my mind buzz. Hard to believe it was written in the Forties; it anticipates by sixty years aspects of the 'Nature writing' of our time. The product of years of stravaiging around in the Cairngorms, that long essay understands and conveys better than anyone the absolute physicality, the immanence of the transcendence that abruptly swoops and plucks you in its hooked talons out of the ordinary and carries you not away from this world but into the beating, unsayable heart of it.

Like MacCaig, she was a wonderful noticer, the kind of noticing that opens a crack into the centre of things.

Between gasps for breath, I urge Andy to read Nan Shepherd. Think Forties Zen, think Neil Gunn, another Scot drawn to marrying a love of the empirical with the transcendent. So Scottish, so rooted, so effortlessly Buddhist before Alan Watts wrote a word . . .

'We're definitely too high,' Peter called back. By now there was no doubt about it. So we contoured round that upper shoulder and at last came over some quartzite scree, and a few hundred feet below, pooled in a tight grey-green corrie, we first saw the Lochan a Choire Ghuirm.

We drop our packs on a little promontory at the north end of the Loch of the Green Corrie and stand there, taking it in.

My first reaction: it's not especially bonnie. Nor is the corrie particularly green. I'd imagined some blue jewel cupped in a verdant setting, a radiant brooch pinned high on the bosom of a noble hill, looking out over a monumental gathering of my favourite mountains. But despite the coarse grass that spurts among the boulders and bedrock, the overall effect is grey and austere.

On three sides, slopes fall steeply to a rough fringe around the lochan. Down the slopes across from us fall shrouds of scree, probably quartzite eroded from the summit. Now the sun has gone in, that grey scree lends the clear water its colour. There are no flowers, no blooming heather, no trees, bushes or bird life. At 1,800 feet, the breeze – from the east of course – is strikingly cool.

If this is the Green Corrie, I think, I'd hate to see the Grey one.

Andy hunkers down at the water's edge, dabbles his fingers in, licks.

'Perfect alkalinity,' he pronounces. 'There are definitely fish in here.'

Often when you meet a friend's new love you look and listen and wonder what the fuss is about. He or she seems perfectly ordinary, one among many. And this seems another Highland loch, a bit more remote and bleak than most. It must have hidden charms. Or maybe it has lots of easy-to-catch fish.

I go through my fly box and pick out a Blue Zulu as the bob fly, the one nearest to me on the cast. A Black Pennel for my tail fly. I select a nameless dowdy bit of fluff as the mid-fly, aware that Peter and Andy already have their lines out. We all want to be the first person to catch Norman's fish. As I tie the flies to the slender, near-translucent gut of the cast, I think of my own AK MacLeod, my old climbing friend.

Even as I assemble my cast, I see Mal Duff's broad, battered fingers, delicate and precise as he calmly improvised his own flies on the kitchen table, the night before a fishing trip. I see how at peace he was, that restless man, at such moments of absorption. I see him teaching me how to cast, standing on a summer evening on the green at Culross, each with a rod and a barbless fly. *My father wouldn't take me fishing until I could cast onto a dinner plate at twenty yards.* Our casts fell harmlessly onto a sea of sunlit grass, I remember, and we went at it for a couple of hours then went home through twilight.

Memory lodges, is barbed, will not pull free.

I attach the cast to the thicker, yellow floating line, using the knot Mal taught me. In this cool breeze there is no sign of any bug life above or on the water. Maybe that's what MacAskill meant by it being no use if the wind's from the east, the chilly direction. And these flies look like nothing that ever flew or swam. I have to trust that trout, like ourselves, rise to metaphor. Or are instinctively curious.

Feeling excited and self-conscious as though we were being watched, I stand on a lichened rock beside the promontory and trail the flies in the water to get them wet and heavy. I can see all the stones on the bottom, never clearer. Andy is already working the shore to my right, Peter on the other side. Their lines roll out straight and silent, drop lightly onto the bright, choppy surface.

My apprenticeship with Mal had been entirely from boats, where casting is less critical. But maybe I'll get lucky. At the very least I'll learn and get better. I murmur *This one's for you* and set the line swirling over the wavelets' light chop.

Retrieve: a light chop

It seems I no longer have to go to the Loch of the Green Corrie to access it. At times it is enough to think on it. Sometimes it is a dark Rorschach blot where I may spy my own projections. Today it is a flattened crystal ball, the light smashed to pieces in the light chop.

Sitting at a table in a writing shed in a wintry garden in Edinburgh, I cast again that line *the light chop*, for in the depths something has twitched.

It is easy to mistake oneself. Families do it for you early on, friends assist later (enemies tend to be more accurate; they get you). 'The quiet one', 'the wild one', 'the sensible one' – the labels are handed out and stick even as she is hollering within, and he yearns to be acceptable, and she is driven to be what she can never be.

Pointless to blame others, you do it to yourself. They do not so much fuck you up, your mum and dad, as give you a wrong account of yourself and let you do the rest.

Calm down, son. The tremble on the surface of those waters, that agitation suggests something more is lurking out there. The three familiar figures spread out round its shores seem to think so too as they innocently, urgently go to it. So draw your arm back, press forward and send line again out with a slightly different twist.

★

How come the bright and dreamy boy knew nothing of himself? How come one morning he caught a bus to Portobello and took all those pills, this clever boy with his Philosophy degree, thinking this made sense, when to stay was intolerable and to leave inconceivable? How come he came to this surrender as he waited for the pills to take effect and watched the cold chop of the waves – I remember, I remember – so leaden and joyless, and what opaque final reckoning went on before he found himself in a phone box fumbling a coin, then lying in the bottom of it curled up as on the bedrock of the seabed, blurry with weeping?

Once in a long while it is necessary to go there again.

The visitors came: parents baffled, wife tearful and outraged, friends the best of whom said 'The question isn't Why but Why Not?' The one you were mad for knitted a Sweater of Many Colours and left it on the bottom of your bed. How many changes of address and circumstance you would wear that through, before it finally unravelled.

The clock on the wall, at times its second hand took minutes to shift. You stared and stared at it in the long silences, thinking this unendurable. How can we sustain ourselves when one minute drags like an hour? The big hand shifts, quivers then settles, and nothing lets up or develops.

Everyone wore slippers, we did our *slip slap slop* pad to the morning sessions, the afternoon evaluations. In between we sat or lay or paced, awaiting deliverance. The anorexic girls huddled together, breastless, hipless, raging. Big John walked with his chest stuck out like a pigeon, head thrown back, muttering people were looking at him, and of course they did because he looked mad. And that wee bloke whose name is lost to me kept running back to the recreation room – how we all needed re-creation! – to lower the needle for the hundredth time on 'Mama We're All Crazee Now'.

The medication trolley squealed; the tea-trolley did not steer well and chipped the walls. We shrank from one, clustered round the other, but at least both were events.

Nights were long as those of doomed polar explorations, marked by cries and mutters, inspections and occasional crises. Once, when you knew you were really sunk, not just clinging to the wreckage till you were carried back to shore, a red-headed nurse sat with you for hours, gripped your hand and talked about her funny, hopeless crushes on straight friends, and the faithless girlfriend whose return she was hanging on for. Her grip and her honest tears were the most healing thing that happened to you there.

Doctor Cox – a Freudian, I trust! – had shiny lace-up shoes, shiny short hair, a clean, blank face and no visible emotional life or gift for empathy. He was an analyst and it was soon clear he could tell you nothing useful. You had done all the analysis you could stand. If thinking got us anywhere, we'd all be enlightened beings by now. Still, he gave you something to encounter and inwardly know *Not this way*, and so in that undersea ward of invertebrates begin to acquire a little backbone.

Then it was March, cold and bleached in the gardens outside, the trees naked and black. In the streets, the shock of so many people when you went with the married anorexic to buy chocolate doughnuts, and sat and ate for two in the little café while she watched in wonder and talked about her good husband, her misery and yearnings. She took a little piece of chocolaty dough in her shrunken white fingers, turned it, sniffed it, put it down. 'Maybe next time,' she said.

The ward guitar had a broken tuning peg. You learned to tune the other strings around the unalterable one, and ended up singing sweet, daft Donovan songs that brought flickers to the blank faces of the ladies after they returned from ECT. If you didn't pull yourself together, you too might go down to the basement and become memory-free. It was an incentive of sorts.

Later, after you had performed in the sessions and finally got irritated enough to convince them you were nearly ready – for most of us arrived passive, sundered, blank – Doctor Cox gave the nod, you collected your few things, pulled on the sweater of many colours, and went out the final glass door into the world, knowing only that what you had tried up to this point had not worked.

Shorn of marriage and prospects, with your neo-brutalist haircut you were, perhaps, not quite thirty. Young enough to start over in this world, old enough to know how fearful and compromised that would be.

Messing up completely may free you from the idea that other people spoil their lives through being stupid, wicked, irresponsible or just lazy. Now you will always be one of those people. Their ache will be yours, and that is something gained from this unholy mess.

There was a girl, of course, the one who guaranteed you could never go back to the wrong life when she held you by the root in a damp country night by the Covenanters memorial. She said 'You think too much – now close your eyes and feel.'

I closed my eyes and got by on feel.

Feeling then became the new, capricious, shifty god that justified many slaughters along with fresh hosannas. Dethroned now, it is possible to see that a feeling, however striking, is still only a feeling. It takes shape, reforms, drifts then goes, just another passing cloud.

So what is real, what persists, if not thought or feeling? Perhaps only sky itself, the space in which all this occurs, opening equally about a real lochan in Assynt and the one attended today, cupped in a high, lonesome corrie of the heart.

Cast: a rise, a bite, a break

We were eager, fresh to the place, wondering who was going to be first for Norman. A single wild brown trout, caught by any one of us, would fulfil our mission, but it would be good to be the one who caught it.

The first ten, the first twenty minutes passed. The sun came full out again. We shrugged off our fleeces and continued. Andy sighed and moved further along the shore; Peter stepped out onto a rock and cast further towards the still centre of the loch. Caught in a swirl of inattention, my cast tangled.

I knelt on the coarse grass, squinted at the pale fine line. Took off my glasses and looked closer – my father's gesture, one I was starting to make more often, like that little grunt when I stood up or sat down.

I got lucky. It was only a fankle, not a bourach – the dowdy mid-fly and the radiant Blue Zulu had involuntarily mated in a tangle of metaphors. I cut off the mid-fly. Keep it simple.

A cry from Andy.

'Rise!'

I looked up in time to see the ripple spread.

'Big one,' Peter called. I got my line out with fresh urgency. It helped to know there was something down there.

Another rise, this time not out in the middle where Peter was casting, but in close.

'Tiddler,' he commented.

Then another. I caught the flicker, then the small slap sound came in on the breeze. It was close in again, in the shallows on Andy's side. He cursed quietly but we were all cheered by the action, and shifted our casts to the shallow margins.

For a long while, nothing much happened. We were busy and occupied with eyes and arms, making the minutes full and empty. Cast and retrieve, working an arc across the water within range, every so often moving along to another stance, another tussock or precarious boulder. We kept an eye on each other, alone in our own patch yet together.

As an hour and then another passed, a sense of the Green Corrie and its lochan began to register, like the image emerging on a Polaroid. Being locked in simple, repetitive activity allows the attention to split, the way you can sometimes do with your eyes. One eye is focused out on water and light; the other drifts inward, to another hillside, another time.

It was a time of black and silver, of muffled panic zipped tight within the leather jacket round the heart. Success was smooth and hard yet breakable as glass. Failure begged from numberless closes. The first Ecstasy smiley badges were slapped on decaying fronts, and it became evident that when the value of property goes up, on the whole that of people goes down. A slight pressure – a missed bus, failing light, an indifferent friend, the voice of Suzy Roche – could bring moisture to my eyes.

Ah yes, the Eighties.

After the partings, tentative reunions, attempts at friendship, the scenes of fondness, guilt, pure need, nostalgia and resentment that had passed between us since she first left, we caught a bus out to the Pentland Hills.

(Let us be truthful. Let this time-telescope not wobble, for the worst things that have happened have been the most valuable. They, not happiness, have brought whatever knowledge we have.)

My ex-lover had been away on a long adventure, not found what she was looking for, and come back single again. We walked for a time then sat near each other among the long grass above the reservoir. When she had finished her story of that man, those places, she glanced at me.

'So it's full circle,' she said.

I knew what was being offered. I breathed in the thin air of the moorland hills, felt the solid ground below, and the open sky above.

'I love you,' I said. Part of me waited, appalled. 'But I don't want you.'

And in the saying, it was true. She looked out over the hills and choppy water, wind shifting her sun-bleached hair. She glanced at me then nodded.

'Yes,' she said. 'Do you think I've something wrong with my heart?'

We walked back to the city, went our ways and never met on that ground again. Had it happened indoors we might have been confused by our bodies, our loneliness, our losses, but out among the hills and water, we said and did right.

It was pretty much it with the Eighties.

This is just daft, I think while extracting a hook from my fishing hat. For years I have mounted into the pulpit of my mind to sermonise passionately on the theme *Being Here Now,* mostly to a congregation of one. Then I sin again, over and over, and live in the past or in anticipation. At one period of my life I risked my neck in big mountains because caught up in the fist of fear and necessity, there was nowhere else to be but here and no other time but now.

So what am I doing here, fishing in the name of a dead man, being flooded by memories? How much more in thrall to the past can one be?

Peter picks his way along the shore towards me.

'It happens sometimes,' he says. 'The loch's gone dead. Still, *if you don't enjoy fishing when you don't catch a fish, you shouldn't be a fisherman.*'

Andy reels in his line. 'It'll get good again later,' he confides as he opens his flask.

We sprawl on the little promontory, eat flapjacks and

drink tea and look at the loch. The sun reappears, the cool wind drops. For a while we just recline and look and no one says anything much.

We are, I believe, entirely happy.

Retrieve: a still point, a turning

Air sidles through heather, mutters over rock and water. The sounds of many invisible oozings gather in the slopes around us, as though we lie within a giant ear. It's what used to happen when the needle came down on the record's empty opening grooves: the sound of presence.

It is an afternoon fit for siesta; lacking shade, we stay awake.

Our surroundings are without trees or shrubs, but there are tiny flowers among the heather. Devoid of animal life, yet we have seen more tiny frogs on the way here. No songbirds but twice a hoodie crow drifted over, offered a harsh *kaak* and was gone. Water shifts on the shore, the coarse grass stirs, clouds re-form even as we assign shapes to them. The world turns and we turn with it, not losing touch.

Peter flips another page of *Love in the Time of Cholera*; Andy flicks at a bluebottle, props himself up on his elbow and stares at the loch as if he could will fish to rise.

The Loch of the Green Corrie is as stripped of decoration as a Free Presbyterian church, yet MacCaig and AK, devout atheists, loved it beyond all other places.

I should have guessed its virtues would be subtle ones. The plainness of this place of water, stone and turf, offers not so much sensory deprivation as amplification. Eyes, ears, the body itself, have to tune to nuance, to the tiny splash of one pink flower, the single distant croak, a ripple where none has been. Perhaps that heightening is what MacCaig so valued here.

Pass a Wee Free kirk in the Outer Isles and faintly hear the psalms in Gaelic: the precentor laying out the line and the distant primal swell of response, neither tuneful nor tuneless – in the way the water on the shore is neither rhythmic nor unrhythmic – is hair-raisingly strange, the sound of something we once knew. Some think the call–response of Black Gospel Music originates here, carried to the Southern States by emigrant Gaels acting as overseers. All too plausible, it being scarcely uncommon for the oppressed to re-establish themselves elsewhere as oppressors.

'Fishing is like hitch-hiking,' Andy announces, gazing at the eventless water. 'After a morning of cars whizzing by, you can't imagine any will ever stop again. But still you have to keep your thumb out and look like you believe.'

Peter glances up from his book. 'Once in Bolivia I completely gave up – and only then did I get a lift.'

Positivity works for some, I think, and the via negativa for others. Hopeful scepticism has long been my predilection.

Andy jumps to his feet. 'I'm going where Ned was, and not moving till I catch something.'

He grabs his rod and sets off. Peter marks his place with a blade of grass and puts Marquez aside for later. He glances at me, that doctor's gaze again: sympathetic, assessing.

'Good luck,' he says. He stretches, picks up his rod and heads along the other shore.

For a while I just sit and watch my friends cast. Whatever we are about here, nothing is gained by hurrying these things.

Cast: a bite, a break, a thrash

I snip off the Blue Zulu – never really believed in that fly anyway, so why would a fish? – and tie on something green and fluffy. I get up stiffly, flex my right shoulder to work off that stab under the shoulder blade, and go back to it again.

If catching a fish here was easy, it would mean less.

An involuntary cry from Peter. As he balances on a rock out in the water, his rod has curved down sharply. Another cry, the rod straightens. His shoulders drop.

'Curses,' he says.

'Big one?' Andy calls.

Peter shrugs.

'So–so.'

'What did you get it on?'

'The Pennel.'

Andy quickly takes in his line and kneels over his fly box.

We fish hard, in silence, keeping an eye on each other. One of Norman MacAskill's few offerings before I left concerned how inventive MacCaig was with barbs and insults when someone failed to land their fish through slowness or in-attention. 'Sometimes in Latin or Greek, which was not fair. Mind you, he lost a few fish himself. Then myself or AK would tell him off in the Gaelic.'

'Did you talk a lot on these trips?' I asked in the hope of more stories.

'No, mostly we fished.'

I'm haunted by the knowledge the three of them came here, as we three are here now, some forty years later. They came here to be in the hills, to fish, to be in each other's company, mostly wordlessly. They would have been the age we are now.

I can almost see their shades quicken in the stir of air over the grass, hear their exchanges in the clack and chuckle of water.

Time passes in cast and retrieve. The lines go out over the expanse, float on it while the cast with its flies slowly sinks. We retrieve smoothly or in little jerks, mimicking food rising. Then arm and rod come back, the line streams overhead. Just before it's fully extended behind, arm and rod come forward; the line flicks, whips then runs out over the water, till the flies drop light as blown seed.

Well, they do for Peter and Andy. My line tends to waver and coil; the flies whack into the surface like little kamikaze bombers. But that's all right. I'm here to learn, pursue and earn the gift of being present.

It's about the right kind of waiting, Mal Duff used to say. Attentive, open, neither impatient nor resigned. Just being there, alert, eyes focused yet looking behind the surface. When it mattered, Malcolm could wait. Boredom and illness he could not cope with; old age and physical infirmity were all he dreaded. Well, he was spared that.

What surfaces now is a long afternoon we fished the

North Third reservoir. He had caught nothing. Even I had landed a couple, returned them. We fished on into dusk, then near-dark.

'If I don't catch a fish in the next ten minutes, I'm going to jump in with my clothes on and swim to the shore.'

After ten barren minutes, with the shore dim and form-less, he sighed, put down his rod, stood up and jumped in.

Mal was not a good swimmer. I rowed ashore, gave him a hand out of the water, drove us home while he sat shivering and puddling. Only a hot shower and a scolding from Liz cheered him up. With red wine in his hand, he was ready to observe 'Andy, good days are earned by all the crap ones – and vice-versa, of course!'

I hear his laugh, his daftness, see the almighty splash he made going in.

Light on water, cloud reflection and sunlight broken on the water. I am beginning to sense the depth of this fluid body, feel the weight of this corrie. Where we are, where this is, gradually become clear. This place is absorbing us. As its lures sink, we are perhaps as much fished as fishing.

The afternoon wears on. My watch is still under my journal back in the tent, but I can sense warmth go out of the day. Then mist crawls down the shoulder of the hill and slithers over the grass. A stiff breeze comes with it, and within minutes wet fingers go white. There have been no more rises. Peter's nibble is as close as we've got to a fish.

With hats and fleeces, we take another tea-break, huddled

out of the breeze. We have covered the entire loch. Nothing is happening out there.

Peter looks out over the leaden water. 'I'm thinking that, like those tramps in *Waiting for Godot*, we have kept our appointment and done our best. We come back tomorrow.'

'Fine, I can be Lucky,' Andy grins. 'One last thrash, then home? Let's really go at it.'

We get stiffly to our feet, flex knees and fingers then pick up our rods and take our stances around the loch. Once again we must stick out our thumbs and look like we believe. By an oversized puddle in a not-so-green corrie, balancing awkwardly on wobbly boulders of belief and hope and doubt, we go at it.

Retrieve: pass it on, pass it on

This is about *transmission*, I think as our three lines go out.
The flies sink from sight, then we retrieve, twitching them
back up towards the surface like subtle memories. The
Dorward casts are economical, the long lines flying back
overhead, the forearm coming forward, the line rolling out
then dropping. Mine are still effortful and meandering.
Towards the end of the day, my wrist burns; someone has
thrust a skean dhu under my right shoulder blade.

Peter and Andy have done this since they were children
and it shows. The knowledge and the love was passed on
by their father. David Dorward may have instructed, but
mostly they were just in his presence when he fished. When
they wanted to start fishing themselves, they had already
absorbed more than they knew. Then they fished nearby
him, absorbing more until they grasped for themselves what
worked and what did not.

When the young writers of my generation sat, listened,
talked and drank with Norman and his peers, we were
getting transmission. It was not one of technique so much
as values.

When Peter said 'If you don't enjoy fishing when you
don't catch a fish, you shouldn't be a fisherman', I can hear
that is his father's transmission. When Andy's eyes light up
as he looks on an unfished loch and says 'I know I can
catch a fish here', that too is his father.

Last night over the last of the Glenmorangie Andy had talked about how, through fishing, his father had tried to show them how to comport themselves. Wordlessly, he demonstrated patience and persistence. Also the necessity of optimism, balanced by realism. Some days fish are not there to catch. If things go wrong − a snagged line, a missed strike, a broken cast − do not blame anything other than yourself. It is natural to get fed up and frustrated, but bad manners to show it. Don't sulk, don't complain, don't *gurn*.

'I suppose that's the way I try to do my job,' Andy had concluded. 'If it works in a burn in the Sidlaws, it should work in Strasbourg and New York.'

I am here to pay homage to those writers who by their humour, openness, seriousness and levity showed us how to comport ourselves. And those parents, friends, old loves and losses by whom we learned − it is time to acknowledge their transmission.

Eight years on, at this table in my shed, I see David Dorward in Ullapool, standing beside his wife Joy on a sunlit corner outside the Argyll Hotel. Hooked pipe unlit in his mouth, grizzled beard, tweed jacket and brogues. Above all I remember his steady manner, at once serious and droll, and the pleasure with which he looked out at the day. Unassuming yet dignified, he struck me as being consciously, almost wilfully old-fashioned, aligning himself with the manners, modes and morals of an earlier time.

Yes, I can see him as a good fisherman. He had the calm alertness, the balanced outlook the pursuit demands. A good man who died well, in so far as anyone can, with his wife Joy and Andy and Peter there, accepting it, his life completed, his knowledge transmitted.

Cast: it's not Bolivia, is it?

Andy trudged round the loch, rod over his shoulder. For a moment he looked downcast.

'Do you think MacCaig is chortling?'

'I'll bet he is.'

'Back to base?'

'Base,' I agreed. 'Food. Wine.'

'Yes!' He waved Peter in. 'I'm absolutely certain we'll do better tomorrow.'

We broke down the rods, stuffed our packs and set off back down the mountain.

Coming over the lip of the bealach we dropped below the mist into butter-yellow evening sunshine. Across the valley, the top of Quinag was sliced off by cloud, but small islands snoozed like curled-up cats in Eddrachillis Bay.

We sat there, letting warmth back into our bones, looking over an Assynt the people owned again.

'Ambition is such a bourach,' Andy said at last. 'Even at school I just wanted to travel and have an interesting time. I looked on the map and thought I'd like to live in Germany and New York. Luckily Andrea did too. Now we have, and that's good. But then I look at this . . .'

He ran his hand over his sweat-damp hair. It was one of those times old friends could voice aloud thoughts, and only then know what they have been thinking, and where they might go next.

'We love New York. Interesting jobs, good friends. But really *this* is what I want.' His arm swept across Quinag and out to the islands. 'Scotland. Fossicking around with old pals. I want more time, and less of everything else. Another year in New York, then if there's the work, we're coming home.'

I see him, sitting at the top of that brae that evening, looking out eagerly into the future. At the time I thought it was just aspiration. But some months after the Twin Towers folded like melting concertinas a few blocks from their offices, he and Andrea moved to London. She began selling rights for HarperCollins; he worked too hard, too many business trips abroad. Enjoyed London, put on weight. After five years of that, he finally returned to where he'd wanted to be: Edinburgh. *The* city.

He still works too hard, has to travel too much, still wants less.

'You never wanted to live abroad, Greigy?' Peter asked.

'I often already do,' I said, thinking of Sheffield.

We sat and silently stared some more at the mountain, the islands, the powder-blue bay. Andy glanced at his brother.

'It's not Bolivia, is it?'

'It certainly is not,' Peter admitted.

'And what about the horseflies, Ned?'

Peter narrowed his eyes and smiled. 'They were the size of helicopters, and could bite through denim *like a dog.*'

We got stiffly to our feet and down we went.

Descent from the Green Corrie

The climb's all right, it's the descent that kills you.
Knees become fists that don't know how to
  clench
And thighs are strings in parallel.
Gravity's still your enemy – it drills you
With your own backbone – it's love is all to
  wrench
You down on screes or boggy asphodel.

And the elation that for a moment fills you
Beside the misty cairn's that lesser thing
A memory of it. It's not
The punishing climb, it's the descent that kills you
However sweetly the valley thrushes sing
And shadows darken with the peace they've
  brought.

Norman MacCaig

Retrieve: oh Graeme, there are other ways

I propped the rod against my tent and carried on round Loch na Gainmhich towards the car. We wanted the wine and whisky left there, and I was at that stage of tiredness when it's as easy to keep going as stop. Possibly I needed a break from the day's companionship. At other times Peter or Andy would quietly withdraw, Peter into his book or Andy for a solitary stroll and stare.

The rough path rounded the loch. In the distance was the black dot of the car. I plodded on.

All day I had been thinking about Norman leaning forward, tapping me on the knee and saying fiercely 'I loved the man! Not like *that*, you understand? But I *loved* him.'

Like many of his generation, Norman had problems with gay men. They made him uneasy, he just didn't get it. So it was all the more striking, that fierce declaration of feeling. He meant what he said: he loved AK Macleod.

'You understand?' And I did, on account of a man I once knew.

He was bulky, shambling, with a big tousled head. His hefty forearms and moth-devoured sweater were streaked with paint. When we first shook hands, his were big and red and fleshy-soft.

He was precariously going out with my girlfriend's school friend. I'd been given to know he was on probation. He had yet to display enough consistency and commitment. Certainly the room he inhabited was a chaos of bottles, roach-filled ashtrays, clothes, books, records, drawings and above all paintings. I inhaled the heady aroma of oil paint, stale beer and hashish: the artistic life, far removed from the domestic order my girlfriend had civilised me to.

He swore freely at things that disappointed or angered him, which often included himself. He talked passionately about Art. His conversation was full of question marks and exclamation marks. He was warm, baffled, hungry to know and understand the world. He was working-class, physical, direct, spontaneous and emotional. He had his culture's gift for anecdote and story-telling. Unadept at a discourse of abstract nouns, he was driven to his own ways of expressing what was inside him, which I found far more eloquent than mine.

Years later I reworked elements of him as Graeme in my first novel *Electric Brae*, and we might as well stick with that name. That book reads now as a kind of elegy, for there are other ways than death to lose a friend.

Graeme had a strong Scottish Central Belt accent. He loved and respected his parents (not so common among artistic types), while breaking with the way they and most of his former friends led their lives. Despite his apparently Bohemian lifestyle, core values remained from his upbringing: honesty, earned respect, community, humour, *work*.

Art was his work, he was no dilettante. Difficult abstract art, big canvases of greys and blacks, heavily cross-hatched and scarred. *Andy, I dinni invent abstraction − I jist transcribe it!*

I didn't get it. I drank the Newcastle Brown, passed the joint, looked at his latest work and listened. So many evenings, with our girlfriends next door conducting their own version of what mattered, Graeme showed me Art books, talked of Expressionists, Abstract Expressionists, Minimalists, Constructivists. All the while there was music: Hendrix, Coltrane, Miles Davis, Weather Report, Captain Beefheart.

He painted in front of me, painted as he talked, took the joint, asked me about things I was supposed to understand – literature, poetry, philosophy, the meaning of life. One thing I could see: his art was not a con or a joke or an evasion. This baffling, problematic, difficult work was utterly and deeply felt. He *meant it*. He threw all of himself, heart and soul – words he had no problem using – into his canvases and conversation.

That commitment, I think now and bless him for it, slowly rubbed off on me.

He made my former school friends appear timid, dull and unadventurous, and my new philosophy and writing friends seem cerebral and colourless. We talked and our conversation went all over. I felt lit up, engaged, charged. He didn't just talk about *things*, Graeme. He talked from his emotional life, his core. He encountered the world full-on with his eyes, his hands and his heart, and he made no attempt to hide it.

Like Norman and AK, we lit each other up.

Of all the stories he presented me, this is the one at the head of the queue today. Graeme was sitting in a farmyard with an early girlfriend one sunny morning, feeling drowsy, laid-back, philosophical. He found himself watching a young blackbird, sitting on a low fence, fledgling feathers lifting and settling in the breeze. He saw the farm cat inching up behind it. It wasn't his place to interfere. The cat went back on its haunches . . .

'Then my girlfriend said *Don't be stupid, man!* and she threw a stone and the bird flew off and the cat went hungry. I realised that's oor nature, having a choice. She was dead right, we are born to interfere. So we do it well.' Pause. 'What d'ye think, Andy?'

Then it was 1977 and his spacey jazz was replaced by shouty din. Punk sounded to me like Rock 'n' Roll had to my parents. But Graeme played it over and over till one night I abruptly registered music and meaning, just as my eyes finally got his difficult, passionate canvases.

Punk had only three chords – in the case of the lovelorn Wreckless Eric, sometimes just two – but at its best they were the right three chords.

I came to love that music's clarion call to anarchic freedom, outrage, experiment, but with university over, the choice now seemed to be between signing on and being a waster, or going straight. 'Facing reality' my girlfriend called it, and I felt she should know.

I got a job as an advertising copywriter, the unglam-orous sort, writing copy for hotels, industrial workwear, smokeless coal. My girlfriend suggested I could keep writing as a hobby. I winced, shrugged. I should have run for the hills.

We had many times together, the four of us. Holidays,

meals, celebrations, arguments, scenes, hilarity. Graeme and I went out fishing together – coarse fishing, just mackerel – in a small tub of a boat neither of us could handle. We walked hills, clambered through scratchy woods, knocked up meals, got woozily high. I loved his company, as he loved mine. I was there when he got married, shook his hand, wondered at the settlement he'd made and thought I should probably go the same way.

And there was that night. There had been wine, then many drinks in the pub across the loch, then back with a bottle of whisky. At some point we realised we'd left some of the carry-out down at the boat. Graeme and I stumbled out into the darkness, blundered giggling through the rhododendrons, slithered and rolled down onto the beach. I tripped over the boat and fell into the bottom of it. I was looking up at the rotating stars, saw his shape bend over the gunwale, that big fuzzy head and shoulders.

It came out of me like a burp needing release.

'I love you, man.'

That was how we spoke back then.

'I know,' he said. He reached out. Grabbed my hand and, as he pulled me out of the boat, he added 'Great, isn't it?'

Then with the bottle we somehow got back to the cottage. It was there and true and nothing more needed said.

My much-debated marriage pleased him. Maybe it validated his own choice.

My subsequent breakdown, separation and divorce – that liberty, that yearning for the right life – he deeply disapproved of, as of course did his wife, who encountered much of my ex-wife's unhappiness. Now it was as though his life was a criticism of mine, and mine a rejection of his. I was embarrassed in his house; he was edgy and dismissive with my young girlfriend.

My life spun out of Edinburgh into relationships, situations and adventures he knew nothing of. He kept making Art for a while, until teaching and children – he took his responsibilities seriously, as he believed a man should – gradually limited his time and energies to what was essential.

I called round a few times, took in the domestic order of their home, heard his latest music, ate their food and gave them an unilluminating account of what I was doing. We were pleasant, awkward, polite. My words sounded like they were being relayed on a playback monitor. *What the hell are you doing, man?* was not said. Nor was *Is this really what you wanted?*

I expect we never again will speak to each other from the heart. Some things can be repaired, others gently put by.

A divorce, if it means anything other than failure, is about tunnelling out of the prison camp we have ourselves made, passing under the wire and escaping through forests of pain and grieving – mostly other people's, don't you forget it – in search of the life you should be leading.

She later married the right man, had children. I met a lot of people, did not. Lovers, allies, consolations, adventures and friends came and went in the life I stumbled through for the next eighteen years. And now there has been falling in love again, so improbable, unmistakable and destabilising, for we become accustomed to our pains and solitudes.

Graeme has the life that is his, and I hope it is good. Once I would have known, for he kept nothing back. We went the different ways that have defined our lives. Mine was the crueller, more selfish one, I have never doubted that. But it was mine and it was necessary.

And that burp, that blurt of love, never repeated? I am glad it was said and understood, for it was true. It also informed the moment a ravaged Norman MacCaig near the end of his long life leaned forward, prodded my knee in fervent emphasis, and said 'I loved that man. You understand?'

As I plod on over the moor, those faces arise, pale husks of themselves, like the moon by day floating over Quinag's flank.

Some people say, some people sing, that they have no regrets or remorse. They must be fools, or more coldly enlightened than I am, or ever want to be.

The interior of the car smelled fousty and a little fruity. Everything was as we'd left it, a strew of clothes, newspaper, food wrappers. I considered putting on the radio to find out what was happening in the world. No, I already know what is happening right here. We try to keep up with everything, everywhere, and just get befuddled and left behind our real life. *He kept up with world events* – what sadder epitaph?

I picked up the wine and whisky, locked the car. Right now in Sheffield Lesley and Leo and Josh would be having their tea, leaning towards each other around the little table. The love she has for her children has no 'wait and see how it turns out'. It is an unnegotiable given. Imagine a bond like that between adults, an end to all these irresolutions. Yet she and I have been up the romance tower too often to look into each other's eyes and jump off the parapet, each believing the other has the parachute.

But certainly you have to jump off something, I thought to her across four hundred miles, then set off back across the moor to my friends.

I have to pull back now and look upon this tired, quietly happy, befuddled man trudging back across the moor towards his friends with alcohol in his arms. What indeed was he waiting for? A burst of celestial trumpets? His life to begin? His lover to get pregnant so he'd finally know what to do with his life?

I can see his convalescence was not complete. Memory lapses apart, he was apparently functioning and strong enough to climb those hills, but he was still something of a husk. Having the brain squashed to half its size by its own fluid inside its own box will always take some getting over.

No, no excuses. He'd long been like that. Yearning and cautious, he believed he could be both spectator and participant. Sweet, earnest blethering idiot, still looking for a way to live without dying, to love without giving over his heart.

Still, watching him turn the corner of the loch and wave

to his waiting friends who are so thirsty for booze and life, I accept he had decent moments and did his perplexed best. He is, after all, on the same pilgrimage I am on, one without sacred relics waiting at the end, except for his own bones. As we lurch on in mutual foolishness, further into the mystery, that will have to do.

Cast: days of Fate & ferret

We lay on the shingle of Loch na Gainmhich. Every so often Peter would scramble back up the bank to check on the stove, where rice, peas and chorizo burbled in the blackened pan. We were tired, leg-weary, at ease. The first whisky was poured into plastic mugs then cut with loch water. We were ready for leisurely talk.

Once I began, and reached out along that branch of memory, I knew which fruit, hidden for so many years, was finally ripe to drop into my hand.

Two euphoric Fife schoolboys went backstage after the gig at the Usher Hall, to meet their heroes the Incredible String Band. They assumed the blazing sincerity of their enthusiasm would get them through any obstacles, and in this case it did. This was 1968 and there was no security at all. The lads wore magpie clothes. Their thoughts, ideals, mythologies and songs were similarly magpied, picked up from anywhere, some from their own backyard, the harbours, caves, neuks and woods of East Fife. Though they scarcely knew it, that was the best of what they had.

Backstage among the raggle-taggle gypsies, clowns, wizards, tricksters and fools, Mike Heron's sizzling grin was too bright and scythe-like to approach. So they wandered over to Robin Williamson. He was sitting on an ordinary chair but still seemed to be *hovering*.

'Hello there,' he said.

Andrew held out a half-drunk bottle of Bulmers cider, for he had no myrrh to offer.

'Would you like some cider, Robin?'

'Aye, thanks.' He took it and drank, twice, then handed it back. 'Sweet apple-ghosts.'

And that, I told Andy and Peter, was how it began. If we wanted to bring our tapes to the Witchseason office, Rose said to ask the tour manager for the address. Fate & ferret (the ampersand, the distribution of upper and lower case, the ambiguity as to who was which, these mattered) went over and introduced themselves. A very tall thin woman with black hair to her hips, cavernous eyes, soaring cheek-bones, long jaw and posh deep voice, smiled on them.

'What kind of songs do you write?'

F&f looked at each other. Where to begin?

'Our own kind,' George said.

If only. Still, she smiled and said 'That *is* good news. Send your tapes and Joe will have a listen.'

Dizzy, dazed, soaring, those small-town country boys went back into the Edinburgh night, clutching that precious address, the ticket to the life that was truly theirs.

Our aspiration was so strong it bent acoustic reality. On our one-track recordings we heard the sound of our aspi-rations and it was noble, quirky, meaningful. Slightly flawed, perhaps – that string I could never quite tune, the faint background call of *George, your tea's ready!* – but we felt those glitches added character.

What did we want so very badly? Acclaim, certainly. Fortune didn't come into it. Nor did girls. One each would do fine. Improbable as it sounds now, in 1968 our real desire was to make unexpected, jubilant songs that would move us and our listeners through a world re-enchanted.

A ludicrous ambition, I know. One that has never entirely left me.

Our first album was, I think, titled *Helping Mrs Monbirth*. The second may have been *Apart/Far & Near*. In 1969 we created the world's first gatefold triple album, *Ferreting About*. George mocked it up in miniature, complete with inserts of lyrics, jokes, poems, photos of us with our pals in silly clothes.

I still like the titles, though the albums, due to some oversight, were never actually recorded and released, and so strictly speaking never quite existed. Still, we dreamed big, and our ambition was for more than ourselves.

(MacCaig and his peers, flyting and political and personal disagreements aside, believed that ambition should be reserved for the poems. The rest was flim-flam, vanity. Poetry was not a career; it was both less and more important than that. This attitude was transmitted to us. I think it changed for Thatcher's children – something of the underlying tone of that period must have tugged into them, like a hook into the trout's under-slung jaw. It was not all sweetness and light then, and not all rancour and ambition now, but some generosity of spirit, an open-handed sharing, has passed away.)

These asides did not appear in the yarn I told the Dorward

brothers as we lay, unhurried, on the shingle in the post-sunset light. The bottle went round, we took what we wanted and passed it on, then I peered back down those years and continued.

A phone call, our small packs and two guitars in plastic covers just in case, then into Jake Fleming's scampi lorry on a wintry Anstruther dawn. Twenty-four hours later, smelling faintly of fish, the life-altering tape in George's duffel coat, we'd get off at Billingsgate, all steaming breath, glinting scales and shouted Cockney incomprehensibilities, and head shivering to the Witchseason Productions office in Wardour Street.

At that time, Joe Boyd managed and recorded the Incredible String Band, Pink Floyd, Fairport Convention, Nick Drake, while running the UFO club, the HQ of London psychedelia. He was very tall, lean, wore cowboy boots and drawled. He was immensely cool, and kind to the odd-smelling boys. I remember with gratitude a lunch he bought us, when we were faint from lack of food.

J. was his assistant, gatekeeper, tour manager, publicist, and our ally. She mothered and protected, indulged, disciplined and encouraged us, as she did so many real musicians. While running the Troubadour in December 1962, she had recognised a skinny kid in boots coming down the stair and said 'You're Bob Dylan, aren't you? You can get in free if you play here next week.' She was the one who offered him his first London gig, who made sure he ate, found him somewhere to sleep. 'Bobby was sweet, driven and very funny,' she said. 'He was good at seeming help-less and women wanted to mother him. He listened and watched, and he learned at incredible speed.'

Like MacCaig, she had her well-worn stories, pearls spun around the grit of truth. Such as sitting with friends in some tea-rooms on Princes Street in Edinburgh, looking out at the Castle while Dylan sat scribbling lyrics to 'Masters of War' on a paper napkin, occasionally breaking off to join the conversation, then writing more. It's just a moment in time, but it sticks in my head: sunshine on the Gardens, the lively group at the window table, and off at the side the scruffy young man with robin's-egg blue eyes and yellowed fingernails, writing furiously as he channels the zeitgeist.

Waiting in the outer office for Joe to call us through and give the verdict on our latest offering, J. would drink tall gins and talk about Paul Simon on his first visit to London, Tom Paxton ('a gentleman, very nice manners'), John Renbourn, Bertie Jansch, and her great loves the Fairports and Sandy Denny. Once a cadaverous young man with long hair and face averted wandered in and just stood by her desk, apparently unable to speak. She nodded.

'In you go, Nick.'

Nick Drake went into Joe's office. We waited some more. In time he came out, looked at us briefly and intensely, then left.

Joe called us in.

The worst was when he played back one of our tapes while we were there. As the reels turned slowly, I heard what he heard in Soho instead of what we'd imagined in Pittenweem. It was horrible. My voice was flat, the mandolin out of tune, the whistle painful. Even the better songs — George's — were risibly badly recorded. The warm-up *Aaahh*, that improvised Indian modal wail with which our more profound songs tended to start, was revealed as a hideously inept imitation of Robin Williamson.

I wanted to leap over the desk and switch off the recorder and run. Instead we sat, sweating, smelling of scampi.

Eventually Joe swung his long legs off the desk and clicked the Stop.

'I kinda like the funny one,' he said.

Back home we'd recover our self-belief, think about our 'new direction', and write more songs. In our last year at school we decided to 'go electric'. We made another tape, mocked up another album and posted it to J., then got on the scampi lorry again.

We bumped into John Martyn in Soho; he was the nephew of our gym teacher and we talked Fife for a while. He said he was playing at Les Cousins that night and we could go on before his spot. We had terrible colds, drank large amounts of cough mixture and felt very peculiar. It was our debut farewell London performance.

On these visits, J. looked after us, as she did many others. When the ISB got into Scientology, F&f would have followed them. But she took us aside and said very firmly 'Don't touch it, boys. It's fascism. Join that and I'll never speak to you again.'

We were astounded. But we listened. And she was right. Once the joyful players had tied themselves to one belief system, they may have been happier but they quickly ceased to be incredible.

She was as adamant about respect and good manners and looking after each other as she was about the importance of fun, mischief, celebration. She took Bobby to a tea-shop in the Isle of Wight and fed him tea and scones, cream and jam because he looked peaky. On tour, Dylan would still phone her randomly from wherever he was in the world, for we don't forget those who were kind and available to us when we were young. He once phoned to complain he was soon going to be fifty and didn't know what to do about it.

'It's very simple, Bobby – you have a big party and ask your friends.'

We don't give up on our dreams so much as locate their more realisable elements. After my first meeting with Norman, I tried to write some poems like my own. In time they began to get published. Between song-writing and rehearsing F&f, I read and wrote more. There were readings, pamphlets, then a first collection. It wasn't *Helping Mrs Monbirth*, but at least it did exist.

You start with what you want to do, and end up with what you can do.

After 1973, F&f went their separate ways. Through marriages and divorces, break-ups of bands, changes of loca-tion, hairstyle, focus and finances, when we met up there was still loyalty to the common ground of the East Neuk of Fife and the daffy days.

I also kept in touch with J. Her office at CBS in Soho was a good place to call in for fun, stimulation, coffee (she stuck to gin) and biscuits on the few occasions I was in London. I enjoyed her energy, style and stories.

Her parents had been prominent left-wing journalists, part of the Soho–Fitzrovia set. As a child she remembered Anna Freud, Sigmund's daughter, calling by, 'very scary and proper, though she gave me chocolate. Clement used to pull my hair when he thought no one was looking. Lucian was frightening even then – he said he wanted to sketch me because he liked my skull. There was another brother called Stephen who used to sit up in the tree and talk to me. I liked him best.'

I sent her my early collections. She assumed because I studied philosophy I must be intelligent. She liked my poetry rather more than my songs. She said she found my company stimulating; I was pleased and flattered because she was legendary.

We had been out for a CBS expense lunch. She gave me her home address and phone number. When evening came I had nowhere to stay in London. I hesitated, then phoned her.

She seduced me, I can see that now. Not that I was unwilling, more that I would never have thought of it. In that car there is always one person driving and one along for the ride.

She was eleven years older though it seemed more. She was much more experienced, moved in another world. I had always looked up to her; now I was being asked to look at her eye-to-eye. The readjustment is never quite complete.

But there was red wine, lots of it. By the big fire in that chilly flat, she switched to gin, her real poison. There was a long joint and a rug by the burning coals. There was Dr Hook's 'Love You a Little Bit More' purring from the speakers. I didn't see what was coming. When I did, I thought I must be mistaken.

In a way I was, but by then it was too late.

We woke. She seemed jaunty, I was dazed. Light was flooding in the back porch onto me as I sat in the deep hip-bath, drank strong coffee while she made omelettes and listened to the Archers Omnibus. I wondered where we went from here. I had been untrue to two people, and one of them was me.

I was, as usual, in a relationship. She said she'd assumed that. She took me into the office and introduced me to her boss. 'This is Andrew – he's straight.' I sat and read trade magazines while she made transatlantic phone calls and had her first gin of the day. I felt out of place, raised, perturbed. I knew I wasn't half as interesting as she said I was. She had another gin, I had another coffee and waited for lunchtime.

Only looking back, I told Andy and Peter, is it clear how little I grasped. For years I'd studied philosophy, got high, read books, listened to clever people and written poetry when it was there to be written, had relationships. 'And still I knew fuck-all about anything that matters.'

It came out strongly, near-tearful, raw. Andy nodded; Peter grimaced. We had another Glenmorangie, Peter checked the stove then came back to hear the finish of the story.

We slept together a few more times, when I was in London, or meeting her on tour. She wrote letters to me Poste Restante. Big cursive fountain-pen writing, purple or green. They started off newsy and funny, became emotional. The writing got bigger and bigger as the stream of consciousness burst its banks. By the last page there was room for only a few giant words, usually invoking *the dark goddess*.

I couldn't say what I felt or wanted. I tried to avoid occasions when it would be possible for us to spend the night together. We never discussed it. There were her erratic letters, and my replies enclosing new poems, philosophy notes and tortuous thoughts. I looked forward, uneasily, to seeing her.

I went once to meet her mother. She was old, upright, dignified, with the same death's-head face as her daughter, but smaller, with long white hair up in a bun. We ate roast pheasant with chestnut stuffing, drank quality claret. I can taste it yet. I slept in a small single bed. J. came to say goodnight, sat on the edge of the bed as we talked. Eventually she got up, passed her hand over my face and wandered out. We never slept together again.

Next day was sunny. We cycled along the lanes of East Anglia, ended up at Aldeburgh. She told me that as a child on a visit during the Festival there, her mother had introduced her to T.S. Eliot and left them together. They had tea and scones. She knew vaguely that he was quite famous but she didn't know why. He showed her how to do 'Cats Cradle' with string, and told her nonsense rhymes. She enjoyed him.

I like to think of that, austere Eliot entertaining a child. And I like to think of that day we spent cycling round East Anglia. She hadn't had a drink that morning, was happy and relaxed, talking about her childhood.

Her mother died of a heart attack while smoking, and in the process burned down the house. When we met next in London, J. seemed gaunt, gutted as the cottage itself. She never got over it. I realised she was not invulnerable. It transpired her mother had forgotten to renew the house insurance. For all the glamour of the music industry, J. had no savings, no property. The cottage was all there had been, she'd intended to retire there.

After a couple of tumbler-sized gins, she told me she had once got pregnant in Ireland, back before the Sixties proper. She had the baby, then gave it away for adoption. She still hoped that one day the grown-up child would find her. I briefly glimpsed the depth of her unhappiness; it went down and down and down, like the long black hair framing her bone-white face.

After that, nothing turned out well. There were no more

Poste Restante letters, just the occasional on-tour postcard. She left work for a long time, lived in one room in the cottage as she tried to make it habitable. I got involved with the Himalayas, she went back to work.

The last time I saw her, she was gaunt, all bone. She talked of recently meeting up with Bobby at a Rolling Stones party in London. They'd agreed it was boring, and left. That night they walked for hours in the rain through the streets of Soho, talking about old times, friends, faces and scenes they had once known, how life stood now. I wish she had set down what was said between them then, but though she loved to tell stories, she had no confidence in her ability to write. I don't know if, behind her vehement front, she had any confidence at all.

I got a postcard. It had been ages since I'd heard from her. It was a Lucian Freud painting. On the back in that big loopy script she had written *Hospital boring as always*. I wrote back, tactfully enquiring about the hospital, but got no answer.

The phone call came just before Hogmanay 1997. J. had been found dead on her bed in the cottage. She had dressed up to go out to a Christmas invitation, must have felt unwell and lain down for a rest. Heart failure, the doctor said, after chronic alcoholism, prolonged depression and malnutrition.

The obituaries made much of her famous friendships. None mentioned the child who had never found her, who probably never knew of her existence. Senior players in the music industry came to the funeral, where surviving members of Fairport Convention sang 'Meet on the Ledge'.

I had failed to see the pattern and meaning of those gins, the long ice-clinking glasses that began mid-morning. I saw her despair only once. She was legendary in her world, the guardian of young Fate & ferret, my only older lover, and she died alone and without money in a half-derelict house. I hate that as much as I want to know what passed between her and Dylan in those hours night-walking the streets of London.

Sitting cross-legged on the shingle in the fading light, I spread my hands helplessly.

'That's it,' I said. 'She was a friend I think I neglected and she is gone.'

We were silent for a while, listening to our own thoughts and the wavelets breaking along the dim shores.

'Well,' Andy said at last, 'let's drink to your friend.'

We chapped our plastic mugs together, a muffled toast, and then passed loch-diluted water of life across our lips.

Out in the November garden outside my shed the summerhouse lies empty. Now no one sits or reads or sleeps there, the spiders' webs have grown thicker and more complex. The once spindly bridges between uprights are now dense grey shawls. So it is with the slender connections, memories, meetings, reflections and micro-narratives that accrue here. The Web is only one strand of the web that connects us, dazzlingly and dizzyingly, to our pasts, our people, our places. At times it seems the Loch of the Green Corrie extends without end; there is no counting the ripples that pass across its surface.

Perhaps this is a book of homages. Perhaps all such books are.

Cast: a small cigar, the poet's ear

Peter took out a small cigar, a treat he allowed himself at times like these. He lit it, drew deeply and exhaled. An ex-smoker since I'd left hospital, I still relished passive smoking, and it kept the midges at bay.

'Stories,' he said. 'The key to general practice is hearing the untold story.' The rim of the cigar glowed red. 'That's where you have to meet the patient.'

'I don't believe my wee brother is a proper doctor,' Andy said. 'Shame he couldn't keep that fish on the hook.'

'I'm not going to rise to that,' Peter retorted. 'Like fish to your casting today.'

'Tomorrow is another day.' A pale flare still lay along the sky beyond the islands as Andy peered at his watch in the gloaming. 'Actually, it nearly isn't. Think I'll turn in and read.'

Glow of head-torches through canvas while Andy and Peter read, the shifting pools of light as though consciousness were moving within the body's tent. I had deliberately not brought any reading with me, and left my radio and Walkman in the car. For these few days I wanted everything first-hand.

I relit the stove and brewed myself a last mug of tea. Zipped up the fleece, pulled on my fishing hat and sat out on the shingle by the glimmering. Not thinking, just noticing.

What came to me was from my last evening with Norman. Once he had shuffled to his chair by the fire, he clearly wasn't getting up again. 'Drink,' he'd said, and pointed. 'Glasses.'

He poured, we drank, then there was silence.

On the mantelpiece, alongside the one of AK, sat a framed photo of four merry, white-haired, distinguished men: Iain Crichton Smith, Norman elegantly adjusting his tie, Seamus Heaney leaning forward with a big smile, youthful in comparison, one arm on Norman, the other on the shoulder of Sorley MacLean, who wears a red waistcoat and a disreputable hat. Standing in a sunlit garden, they could be the elderly wandering monks idealised in Chinese paintings, though in their pleasure at being together they seem more like a mischievous schoolboy gang.

Norman cleared his throat. 'Seamus was getting his honorary degree from Stirling that day,' he said huskily. 'He decided to ask along his pals.'

He sipped, swallowed without much pleasure. I thought of my father doing the same in the last months of his life, then turning to me and saying 'I've had enough. I've even stopped enjoying this.' He'd said it straight and plain.

Norman was working away in the pocket of his jacket. 'I need you to help me,' he said.

He produced a hearing aid. I leaned over him and fumbled to fit the earpiece. He sat patiently, staring straight ahead. I had to hold his ear away from his temple with one hand to work the clip in behind it. Handshakes apart, I had never touched Norman in my life. It was particularly intimate, feeling his warm, soft ear-skin between my fingers.

He sat back. 'That's better. Now we can have a conversation – though I expect I'll say the same old things.'

I sat watching the last diffusion of light on the water. His skull had been warm against the back of my fingers. *The poet's ear*, I thought. *I could do with that.*

There had been something dreadful in his patient passivity as I'd fitted his hearing aid with awkward reverence. Norman in his pomp never asked for help, any more than he would have shared private emotion. Now loss, weakness and age had reduced him to this raw self. I had thought *reduced*, but I wonder now if *raised* or *freed* might be more it.

He had already spoken warmly of his health-care visitor – *a nice-looking woman, very kind* – and his children's and granddaughter's visits. *They are a great help.* Easy to see it as humiliating, such dependency admitted, the food brought by a helpful stranger doing her job, the young colleague fumbling with your ear, yet it may be that in the acceptance of it we are ennobled as much as reduced. In that stripping bare, living is truly revealed, radiant and frightful.

In a late interview Norman admitted 'I have a long streak of reticence in me', and added that in some way he was grateful to his losses. They had forced him to be more open with his emotions, and he now saw that as a gain.

I think he meant both in his life and in his poetry. Wonderful though his mid-period poems can be, the self-protecting intellect sometimes cut in too soon, the conjuring imagination hid the dark lady, the wit pulled the poem's rug away. In his Late Style, this seldom happens. In fact *style* has no outward show left; the poem walks naked, kept upright only by its necessity.

I drained the cooling tea but did not turn in yet. I was near my friends whose lights had now gone out, and true darkness would not come tonight. In that security it was possible to sit and feel things as they are.

I never touched my own father as intimately, never felt his warm skull through thin hair. Only once as an adult did I hold his hand, that last time in hospital when he began to panic and my mother ran for a nurse, and I gripped his right hand between my two, and said *It's all right, Dad, it's all right* until the nurse came.

I stared at the loch and the dark bulk of Quinag till my eyes ached. Willed the pupils to open wider and see more. Ten minutes later my old man had recovered his composure. As I left he raised his right arm a little from the blankets. *Thank you for coming to see me.*

My father died that night. His last words to me had been uncharacteristic and simple. I had not thought of them for a long time.

The hearing aid installed, Norman told the old tales, polished as a newel post by many passing hands. Sorley MacLean mistaking a hotel hairdryer for a telephone. MacDiarmid standing at the fireplace and saying 'Why have I been writing rubbish all these years?' To which Norman had replied

'Maybe it was when you fell off that tram in Lime Street, Chris – perhaps it damaged your rhythm centres.' And Chris Grieve opined 'No, I think it was when my first wife left me. I lost my Muse.'

Then Norman leaned forward in his chair by the fire and stared at me, almost aggressively.

'What matters to you, Andrew? What do you really care about?'

Never before had he asked me something so personal. From my default position as admiring, curious company for a great poet and icon at the end of his days, I was jolted into the truth.

'Writing,' I said. He nodded slightly, as though that was correct but obvious.

'And?' he challenged.

'Love,' I added. His eyebrows twitched, but he said nothing. 'And landscape,' I added. 'I mean, being outdoors, in it, in certain places.'

He stared at me longer, but I had nothing more to say. However lame or vague-sounding, it had come from the heart.

I picture him looking at me still, those deep-set eyes, that pouting lizard mouth. This was not the 'comfortable, easy-oasy and jocose' MacCaig, but something emotional, primal, bared. His eyes swivelled off to the side, to somewhere I couldn't follow even if I'd wanted to. When they returned, he leaned back in his chair.

'Yes,' he said. 'Not far off the mark.' Then he added, as if in answer to an off-stage question, 'All my life I've been bombarded with things that are lovable.'

That was when I'd impulsively asked him a personal question in return.

'What is your favourite spot on Earth, Norman?'

And thus my sitting here by the shore of Loch na Gainmhich around midnight, dew and memory settling their thousand tiny pinpricks out of empty air.

I washed my face in the loch, cleaned my teeth and went to bed. I thought already it was getting a little lighter.

DAY 3

Cast: a Metaphysical Policeman calls

We were sitting cross-legged over late breakfast, watching clouds gather on the tops, when we saw a black dot moving over the moor in our direction. The dot became a person, the first we had seen since our arrival. The person became, with certainty, a policeman. Moving fast, on the path that led only to us.

We looked at each other. Hide the rods? Too late. Or was he bringing us something worse, like family news?

The policeman rounded the corner of the loch, came up the slight rise. In light of what happened next, I will not describe him.

He stood looking down at us where we sat by the stove.

'Good morning.'

'Grand morning!' we enthused.

He pointed back the way he'd come.

'Is that your car? The black Audi?'

'It's mine,' I said. 'Is there a problem with it?'

He looked at me, at all of us, assessing.

'Not as such,' he said. 'It's been there three days, so I wondered . . .'

'We thought it would be safe enough.'

'It should be, right enough.' His eyes drifted over us, our tents, Peter's rod leaned up against the bank, my landing net. He was in no hurry at all.

'Fishing?'

'Well, camping and hill-walking – and maybe a bit of fishing. It's all right to camp here?'

'You'll have permits?'

We looked at each other.

'No,' I said. 'Do you need them for the hill lochs?'

'You need them for all the lochs.'

'Ah.'

He nodded at the loch. 'Had any luck here?'

'Just some tiddlers,' Peter said.

He nodded. 'Naebody catches good fish in this loch.'

'We really came to fish at the Loch of the Green Corrie,' I put in.

Our policeman considered this.

'That's a fair climb,' he said.

'It certainly is!'

Peter leaned forward, Italian coffee maker in his hand.

'Would you like some coffee? Espresso?'

The morning hung in the balance.

'Aye, thank you.'

While Peter busied himself, the policeman sat down on a rock, took off his hat and ran his fingers through his hair.

'The keepers and local people seldom bother going as high as the Green Corrie,' he said. 'You could fish there for a week and not see anyone.' A pause made itself comfortable. 'Any success?'

'Lost one,' Peter said. 'Medium size. There were a few rises, then nothing.'

The policeman nodded. 'Wind from the east,' he said. 'When it gets cold like that, that loch goes dead.'

'Norman MacAskill said the same.'

He considered the little credential I'd offered.

'Aye well, he should know. He'll have told you to get permits?'

'He did,' I admitted, not wanting to get Mr MacAskill into trouble. 'We went to the Inchnadamph Hotel but it was dead.'

He chuckled, turned the cap in his hand.

'That doesna surprise me.'

The coffee maker spouted, chugged, hissed. The policeman took the mug, sniffed and sipped.

'Good coffee,' he said. 'Strong.' He fumbled in his breast pocket. Andy beat him to it.

'Would you like a roll-up?'

When he accepted, our shoulders dropped, our jollity and innocence became less forced. Suddenly it was very pleasant, sitting by the lochside across the way from Quinag, on a weekday morning, drinking strong coffee in weak sunlight. Kings do not have it better.

The conversation passed to the Assynt Community Buy-out. A grand thing, the policeman agreed. Perhaps it was now more . . . worthwhile to get permits. He scratched his head and admitted he wasn't sure which estate the Green Corrie fell in. It might still be one of Lord Vestey's. Nevertheless . . .

'We'll certainly get permits, next time,' Andy said in his *Trust me, I'm a Scottish businessman* voice.

'Aye, best do that. Next time.'

We got the message.

'It would be better not to fish in sight of the road,' he said. 'Especially on the Sunday – though I've long thought that was a piece of nonsense invented by the landowners to keep the riff-raff from coming up from Glasgow for the weekend.'

My God, we had a Marxist policeman on our hands.

He drained his coffee and looked about appreciatively. Tarnished-silver rain cloud had settled in higher up, slicing the top off Quinag and the hill behind us. It made the broken sunlight brighter, out on the loch and the far islands.

'All right for some,' he said, and got to his feet. 'Were you to fish in the high lochs, I could know nothing about it.' He fitted his cap, tugged the peak down. 'Permits next time.'

As he walked away, he called 'Good luck!' then bobbed off across the moor.

We christened him *the Metaphysical Policeman* because he had come to forgive us in advance for sins he did not consider as such, while making us acknowledge they still had to be pardoned. G.K. Chesterton would have appreciated him; most in the Gaeltachd, including many a Free Presbyterian, would have approved.

As for Lord Vestey, he did not live here enough to count.

We watched the figure grow tiny. The day was ours again.

'Another coffee, I think,' Peter said cheerfully, and bent over the little blackened beast.

Behind what hills does happiness hide, to lurk and plot its return? The Metaphysical Policeman's departure left gusts of entertainment behind, along with rain clouds rolling down the glen. We had become unused to people. Already he seemed like our invention.

Drizzle swept down the slope behind us. The far side of the loch darkened, tin-tacked with rain (another MacCaig image, they were everywhere) and drove us into my tent.

We sat cross-legged, sipping coffee and listening to rain on tent. Peering into my coffee, I wished I still smoked. I could taste that roll-up. It had been sixteen months since I'd stopped, ever since I'd left hospital, shaky and hollowed out but still alive. These sudden, fervent gusts of longing still lurked to ambush me. The first of the day was always the sweetest; the others had become mostly habit and necessity.

'What do you reckon?' Andy said. He knelt at the entrance, looking out at the sky.

'Where's the wind coming from?'

'The east. MacCaig will be chortling.'

'I imagine he is.'

Considering he was dead and gone, Norman was very present. He didn't believe in the place from which he said he would be looking down on our efforts. We agreed we didn't either, but we kept invoking it. The afterlife is perhaps a necessary fiction, the vanishing point by which perspective is created.

Peter put his coffee mug aside.

'I don't believe in an afterlife,' he said. 'But I affect some people, especially Deborah and Jack and Jamie, and that will persist long after I'm gone. That's immortality enough for me, one worth trying to do good for.'

'It must be such a hostage to fortune, having children,' I said. 'Lesley said she'd never recover if something happened to one of hers.'

She had also said if stepping in front of a bullet or a train meant saving Joe or Josh or Leo, she would do it without hesitation. She was not being rhetorical. That still haunted me. It seemed lovers, spouses, friends were all contingent, next to one's children.

Peter nodded. 'Yet the measure of a person's life is how many hostages to fortune he or she is prepared to take on.'

At those words, I felt something shift in me.

The image I have now is of some complex, recalcitrant inner machinery. Clogged by its own age and haphazard development, its rusty parts and complexity, from time to time it lurches forward.

Giving up smoking had had several preliminary stages before something finally shifted, sprockets turned, a lever shot back – and only then was it possible to never light another cigarette. I can see now what the fankled machinery of my life was inching towards that time we came to the Green Corrie; at the time I merely noted something had happened at Peter's words, as though some as yet unknown reconfiguration had just become more possible.

In the short term, our day was rearranged. Rain clouds had set in at about fifteen hundred feet. In those conditions, with the wind still from the east, the prospect of slogging back up to the Green Corrie for another day's unproductive fishing was not appealing.

But down at our level, rain cleared to drizzle then watery sunshine. We couldn't sit about all day. I wanted to revisit certain places for the first time in nearly forty years; Peter and Andy would go stravaiging along the lochans that lie along the fault line running west from Loch Assynt, with rods in packs just in case the mood took them.

We zipped up our tents and set off on the track over the moor.

Retrieve: a toast to James Hutton

It's a rare day when I have nothing to do and nowhere to be. It should happen more often, being self-employed, but my boss is an anxious tyrant who labours under the conviction the company has constantly to justify its existence.

But not today. I dropped off Andy and Peter at the track near Lochassynt Lodge. Rods discreetly broken down inside their packs, with a wave they set off into sun and rain to explore the series of lochans that follow the fault line out to the coast.

I stood by the car, enjoying the solitude, in objective mood after yesterday's rampant subjectivity.

From this side, its scree-torn ramparts towering into cloud, Quinag looked magnificently ravaged. I tried to contemplate the size and force and depth of the glaciers that had enveloped this terrain and then torn it apart in their leaving. Only fifteen thousand years ago, the latest though probably not the last of a series of Ice Ages.

There is evidence that much of the planet has been subject to glaciation. At other times it has been much, much hotter. The notion of our planet as a naturally stable, friendly-to-life environment, a motherly Gaia embracing us, is as daft as the belief we run it. Even the advent of chlorophyll plants and trees killed off a great portion of life on Earth as they pumped the poison of oxygen into the carbon dioxide atmosphere those early organisms depended on.

The planet's indifference and inherent instability is our context. Massive, inexorable changes, rapid or incremental, have happened many times before, and will again.

So old, so old, I was thinking as I got into the car, knowing now where I had to go.

To my father the advancement of scientific method, with its elevation of reason and evidence over tradition, authority, superstition, wishful or magical thinking, was a noble cause, one he invested with emotional, almost political, significance. Evidence was available to anyone with eyes to see, and Reason to anyone prepared to make some effort to think. However flawed by human egos, self-interest, inertia, personal animosity and timorousness, the growth of human knowledge through science was an uplifting story, one in which, unlike in the world, good theory would always finally triumph over bad.

My father had no heroes but he greatly respected people who, through rational argument based on detailed observation, overthrew orthodoxies backed by those with social power and prestige. If they were Scots and from fairly humble backgrounds, so much the better.

So as children he took us to Cromarty to see the birthplace of Hugh Miller, stonemason and paleontologist, author of *The Old Red Sandstone*. He spoke with feeling about Miller's diligence, the imaginative theorising backed up by solid observation that added much to fossil theory and geology. And it was on that trip − I could as well say 'pilgrimage' − my father first mentioned another name:

James Hutton, recognised as the founder of modern geology, one of the men who made *The Origin of Species* possible, the person who took us to the brink of Deep Time and invited us to look down.

There are few more important stories to own than that of the physical planet we live on. These hills, lochs, ridges, seas, cliffs, deserts, fossils and glaciers call, however mutely, *How come?* As do the Earth's events, the floods, eruptions, tidal waves, landslides. What is the history of our world, how old is it, how come it is as it is, where is it heading?

In the religions of the Word – Judaism, Christianity, Islam – that narrative was owned by Genesis. It was upheld and enforced by the Church, which underpinned the State.

The Copernican revolution, which through reason allied to detailed observation finally overthrew the Earth-centric model of the solar system, was accomplished only after huge resistance from Church and State, even though the Bible never actually stated the sun went round the Earth – that was Aquinas's late addition. But chronology is built into the Bible.

Because the Old Testament claimed to be a complete account of the history of the Jewish people from Creation onwards, generation by generation, it was possible to attempt to date the Creation. The King James Bible carried in its margins the dates of the events it recounts, starting with Creation in 4004 BC. This idea had sunk deeply into the European psyche, to the point where querying it would appear absurd, crackpot. Even Newton did not question it.

Another investment theologians had in chronology: the attempt to determine the date of the Second Coming. Martin Luther's dating of the End gave his followers 150 years to prepare.

So the carefully worded conclusion of James Hutton's *Theory of the Earth* in 1795 is incendiary on two counts, and in a time when Creationism is attempting a comeback, deserves to be nailed up in letters of fire:

In respect of human observation, this world has neither a beginning nor an end.

James Hutton trained at Edinburgh University in law, chemistry and medicine – subjects that elevate observation and clear thought over metaphysics. This devoted empiricism, this looking and reasoning without preconceptions at how things are, is the driving principle of the Scottish Enlightenment of the latter eighteenth century.

Influenced by Newton and Locke, these were all empirically minded people who looked for an explanatory mechanism in their inquiries – in social studies (Adam Ferguson), economics (Adam Smith), chemistry (Joseph Bell), human nature, history and philosophy (David Hume). Without a mechanism one had only a *What* but not a *How*. (*Why* they left with a wry shrug to the metaphysicians, those who argued from set first principles – usually arrived at by appeal to some authority or tradition, rather than from observation.)

Previous explanations for rock and land formations had been based on notions of the Creation, later followed by the Flood, or the Universal Ocean. As the waters retreated, limestones and sandstones were deposited in sedimentary layers. Rock that was unmistakably volcanic in origin, granite for instance, had to be earlier, dating from the Creation. Erosion might well affect the land around us, but it worked on a given, not as part of a dynamic.

These theories had lovely names, *Neptunism* and *Catastrophism*, and tried very hard to square Genesis with observable fact – like those gleaming, increasingly intricate brass models that attempted to uphold an Earth–centred cosmology while conforming to astronomical observation. So ingenious, so wrong.

(Once my friend Brian went out to his car in the dark while the person he had called on finished cooking the tea. When Brian came back in he was amazed at the changes: his host had hung pictures on the wall, lit the fire, covered the table in a cloth, laid it, opened a bottle of wine – all in ten minutes! He'd even added a vase of flowers against which was propped a note: *I love you.* Brian was impressed then flabbergasted then alarmed. Only when an equally alarmed stranger came out of the kitchen did he understand he'd come back into the wrong house. We fabricate ever more elaborate explanations before finally admitting our premise is wrong.)

After his studies, Hutton bought a farm in the Scottish Borders and lived on it for a decade. There he was struck by erosion, how quickly soil was carried off, how deep a new run-off channel could become. Even the solid rock of the nearby coastal cliffs could fall apart overnight, fresh boulders adding to those at the base of the cliffs. The land itself could be eaten away, and deposited elsewhere.

His active participation in the surveying and digging of the Forth–Clyde canal gave him further detailed geological data. His close friendship with the great chemist Joseph Black (who was also David Hume's doctor, attending his deathbed) gave rise to the notion of mineralisation of rock, created by extreme heat and pressure. He came to consider granite not to be the original Primary rock from the Creation, but a much later igneous intrusion forced by great heat from below – what else could explain those sites where granite seamed through or lay on top of those sedimentary layers?

He noted instances of what (with unconscious prescience) were called *unconformities*, where rocks of what appeared to be completely different formations and ages were jammed together. The granddaddy of unconformities is at Siccar Point, on the coast not that far from his farm.

Siccar Point is as spectacular as it is intellectually significant. There a layer of red sandstone sits directly on top of hard 'greywacke', a completely different sandstone, one that is tilted up to near vertical, bits of which actually run right through the red sandstone above. How on Earth was a single post-Flood sedimentation supposed to explain this?

By 1765, Hutton had arrived at two core principals: i) most (but not all) rocks are sedimentary in origin, laid down by erosion of older landmasses ii) erosion is universal and constant. What had shaped the planet was shaping it now.

The latter became known as Uniformatarianism – *in the present as in the past.*

Not one Flood, but many floods. Not one Catastrophe but many catastrophes. The killer phrase in his first paper, delivered to his peers and friends at the Royal Society of Edinburgh in 1785 was this: *We find no vestige of a beginning – no prospect of an end.*

He had arrived at a mechanism and a context that still remain the cornerstones of geology. The mechanism was the cycle of Erosion, Sedimentation followed by consolidation and often Metamorphosis through heat and pressure, fresh Uplift through volcanic activity and forces from below. This cycle was driven by subterranean heat. All of these were common, observable, constant processes, *in the present as in the past.*

The context was the Earth's great age. The layering of different strata (pierced at times with intrusions from below), the late appearance of fossils of ever-increasing complexity, which suggested alternating periods of ocean, desert, fertile land, great lakes, all spoke silently of a planet a great deal older than six thousand years.

Just how old, Hutton wasn't going to speculate, for that would be going beyond the observable. As it happens he was a Deist, quite prepared to assent to the notion of a Creator who had set this material and these mechanisms in motion. That was the realm of metaphysics and religion; he confined himself to science.

Hutton delivered his revolutionary theory to the Royal Society of Edinburgh in 1785. At first it created little stir.

He did further significant field studies to establish more corroborating evidence for his argument. Following a serious illness and equally life-threatening operation without anaesthetics in 1791, he worked on in great pain and finally published two volumes of his (garbled and hard to read) *Theory of Earth* in 1795, then died. In his absence his opponents in the Church and the universities misrepresented, ridiculed and suppressed his work.

Those who were prepared actually to look at the evidence had to insist that the basalt sills of Salisbury Crags, despite all logic and observation, in fact pre-dated the rock they rose through. They had to close their eyes to Siccar Point and other unconformities. A whole school of 'Biblical geologists' attempted with ever more bizarre contortions to defend the indefensible.

James Hutton was buried in Greyfriars kirkyard in 1797, near a far more famous dog who arrived a hundred years later, and he quickly became obscure. His argument languished for two generations until it was expanded on by Charles Lyell, after more detailed fieldwork in granite intrusions, in *Principles of Geology* in 1830. Lyell replaced the intellectual monstrosities of Creationism, Neptunism, Catastrophism with a Hutton-based model wherein past change and present circumstance were 'brought about by the slow agency of existing causes'. He went further than Hutton in suggesting the Earth must be old, really really old, old beyond knowing.

The first book the young, curious, ambitious botanist Charles Darwin read on the voyage of the *Beagle* was Lyell's.

Because Darwin had been lectured in geology at Edinburgh University by one of Hutton's principal denigrators, Robert Jameson, he found Lyell's argument startling but interesting. Then he went ashore at St Jago in the Cape Verde Islands, the *Beagle*'s first port of call, and there found a perfectly preserved raised sedimentary stratum.

From that day on, Darwin wrote to friends, he became a convert to Lyell, and thus to Hutton. Now he had Deep Time as a context, without which the notion of the evolution of species through natural mutation and selection cannot work.

As I passed through Elphin amid a land whose Lewisian gneiss bedrock was now gleaming wetly under bright sun, I raised my inward glass to an unsung hero, James Hutton.

Notations of ten summer minutes

A boy skips flat stones out to sea – each does fine
till a small wave meets it head on and swallows it.
The boy will do the same.

The schoolmaster stands looking out the window
with one Latin eye and one Greek one.
A boat rounds the point in Gaelic.

Out of the shop comes a stream
of Omo, Weetabix, BiSoDol tablets and a man
with a pocket shaped like a whisky bottle.

Lord V. walks by with the village in his pocket.
Angus walks by
spending the village into the air.

A melodeon is wheezing a clear-throated jig
on the deck of the Arcadia. On the shore hills Pan
cocks a hairy ear; and falls asleep again.

The ten minutes are up, except they aren't.
I leave the village, except I don't.
The jig fades to silence, except it doesn't.

Norman MacCaig

Cast: touching the Highland Controversy

I parked the car a few miles south of Elphin. Cul Mor and Cul Beag across the valley had been smeared away by the mist's chalk-duster. On this side, sun and drizzle conceived a sharply arched rainbow and a dimmer one outside it, with the colour spectrum reversed. Newton's optics did not make it less wondrous.

By the time I got the camera out, the rainbows had gone, reminding me of the two aspects of Time we live through. Then I climbed the muddy path up to Knockan Crag, battleground of 'The Highland Controversy'.

Standing at the bottom of the escarpment, I ran my hand over the exposed rock. The upper strata were dark, damp and fine-grained, some kind of metamorphic rock, packed with mica and quartz. The lower bands were pale limestone, a different texture altogether, cooler to the touch. They are also, according to my father nearly fifty years ago, now backed up by the information boards nearby, roughly five hundred million years younger than the ones immediately above them.

Yes, *younger*. Here fossil-free Pre-Cambrian rock lies on top of Cambrian. My hand moved wonderingly over the enigma of the Moine Thrust, the heart of the Highland Controversy that made this distant corner of Scotland into the most investigated, most hotly debated, most famous geological site on Earth. This was where, a century after

Hutton, further key principles of geology were hammered out.

But only after a prolonged, bitter and very public struggle of egos, influence and entrenched positions. The most influential geologist of his day, the splendiferously named Roderick Impey Murchison, director general of the Geological Survey no less, insisted that these dark upper rocks – now known as mylonites, formed by intense shearing of even older rock known, rather wonderfully, as the *moine schists* – were more recent than those beneath them. Which meant insisting, in the face of evidence, that they were also of Cambrian age.

Murchison had 'common sense' on his side, as did those who insisted that the sun goes round the Earth. One of my father's *bêtes noires*, Murchison had also invested his career, his name and his authority on it, and he clung to that position in the face of increasing evidence to the contrary. He had a young protégé, James Geikie. A colleague of Geikie, James Nicol, after exhaustive field trips to Assynt, concluded that these upper rocks were indeed Pre-Cambrian and had been forced over the lower rock in the course of thrusting or faulting movement across many miles.

For this heresy James Nicol was rubbished, ridiculed and misrepresented by Murchison and Geikie, and died nearly forgotten and unrecognised.

The Highland Controversy reached its height in the last two decades of the nineteenth century. More detailed field-work in Assynt – which by this time was infested by geologists; it's a wonder any of it remains undemolished by their hammers – by Charles Lapworth and Charles Callaway called Murchison's interpretation into question. This did not go down well with the establishment, who tried to dismiss them as 'amateurs', i.e. not part of the Geological Survey.

Geikie then appointed the luminously named Ben Peach and John Horne to look once again at the Moine Thrust. In 1897 they concluded that Nicol had been correct, that the geology of Assynt was not continuous but riven by thrusts and faults and intrusions, and that the older mylonites on show at Knockan Crag had been forced from many miles to the east, up against and then over the later Cambrian. This was the first clear demonstration of the notion of tectonics, the understanding that parts of the Earth's crust could move remarkable distances, often reconstituting in the process.

Moving along the crag then taking the path up over the top of it, I had some sympathy with Murchison. In places the upper exposed rock is banded into what look like sedimentary layers, deposited later than the limestone below, as common sense dictates. But my brother David, who was there that day fifty years ago when our father took us to see the Moine Thrust, and later became a geologist himself, tells me these banded layers are in fact heavily deformed metamorphic rock. The heat and pressure of the thrust were so great that they produced banding and streaking, totally unrelated to sedimentary layering. The long pale lines under my fingers are pebbles that have been dragged out, as though they were plasticine not solid rock.

*

My father took his children to the Knockan Crag as though to the site of an ancient, decisive battle, and in some ways that is what it was.

I ambled back down to the car and drove off into the rest of the day, floating on Deep Time. I sometimes think only the unfolding present moment and Deep Time are good for us, and better not to mess with mister inbetween. As with the bifocal lenses I tried last year – the close-up and the long distance are true, while the middle distance is fuzzy and befuddled. Unfortunately that is where we live most of the time.

But not today! Across the valley, Cul Mor and Cul Beag had reappeared, with the cloud-hidden upper reaches of Bhein Mhor Coigach to the south, and Suilven and Canisp soared and strutted in the distance, radiant with sun and rain. Assynt looks extraordinary because it is.

I had another five hours before picking up the Dorwards. I carried on driving along on empty roads winding among improbable mountains, to find out where they would take me.

Retrieve: a dub

I cannot remember now where that lochan was, so small it was what my father called a *dub*. A pond, a pool, a puddle. I doubt if I could find it again. My only photo shows a densely wooded slope in the background, and an unidentifiable ridge rising in the distance, so it must have been fairly low down.

Possibly it is by the lovely single-track road that winds and dips out of Lochinver to Clachtoll and Stoer, for there is some woodland there.

Or maybe it is somewhere near Glencanisp Lodge, off the dead-end road that becomes a track that leads below Suilven, right through to Elphin.

Or it could be found on the road which on that day and on many others seemed the most beautiful – that is the simplest word, I'm afraid, for that quality that enters by the eyes to hit where the ribs divide, making us gasp involuntarily – road in Scotland. I mean the narrow, humble, unnumbered road that unspools, elliptical and unhurried as a Sorley MacLean sentence, from Lochinver past Inverkirkaig where MacCaig spent so many summers, where AK lived and died, then twisting, rising, hiding and revealing bays, inlets, lochans, past the two houses at Rhegreanoch, on over the hill where you may crick your neck trying to keep an eye on the road and look simultaneously upon Enard Bay on one side and the glittering sprawl of Loch Sionascaig

on the other, then down to Badnagyle on the long drift
to Achiltibuie and the Summer Isles.

The dub I sat beside could have been in any of these
places, for I passed them all that day, filling my eyes with
light and water, bays and mountains, rainbows and sunshine,
colour from darkest slate to acid lime green. I would not
have thought there was room enough inside, for so much
to come in through the eyes.

The little lochans of Assynt are sprinkled over the moor
like bits of broken windshield. Many bear water lilies; when
they flower I think of miniature white lotus blooms, images
of a particularly Scottish enlightenment, small, discreet,
intense.

There are only so many of them you can bear to pass
by. I got out of the car with no purpose in mind.

I sat on a dry rock, opened my flask, peeled back a
chocolate biscuit bar. Sitting out of the breeze, the sun was
warm on my neck and arms, multiplied itself on the water.
Pink rock orchids shook among coarse, spindly grass. A
strew of small boulders, moss-blotched, scattered in the shallows. In the middle, a tiny island sprouted a spindly rowan
sapling.

It was not just the sight, but the smell. The feel. The
sound.

I would say it was silent but it was not. Wind and water
can never be silent. I would say – and probably did to
myself, so habituated are we – that the world stopped, but
it was more that, like a roundabout turning in the park, I
finally got on it.

For a long time, the kind that makes Time a nonsense or a friend, I sat there.

There was scalding tea, chocolate biscuit, warm arms, clouds moving in the sky and on water. There were clumps of slim reeds like green aerials. When the wind gusted, they leaned, sprung back, leaned again. They drew me into their quivering till only the reeds and their movement remained.

The reeds shook and leaned, responding to unseen signals. The air was full of transmissions, in the wind itself, in radio and television waves, gamma rays, background radiation. In history too, coming off that low rickle of stones above the far bank. The future may have been signalling back as well, for some mind-blown cosmologists suggest Time may move in more than one direction. The reeds bent and received them all, as I did.

And like aerials, the reeds transmitted as well as received. In their shiver and whip, they sent out energy. They took the wind and passed it on, slightly altering the world, slightly altered by it, irrevocably in it. As are we.

I sat there long past my tea going cold, riddled with Assynt, feeling the dub flow into and out of me with every breath, heartbeat and flicker of the eye – receiver and trans- mitter, actor and audience, wide open in this world.

Today I write about it, which is not the same, and you read, which is not the same. And yet. And yet we bend in the wind, moving along the street among our fellow nodding aerials, transmitting and receiving, and just in the thinking of it a lightness comes again.

Cast: the Assynt buy-out

Through that day of sun and shower and mountains piled up like dark cumuli, I drove, stopped, got out, drove again. I must have covered most of Assynt, not clear what I was looking for but absorbed in looking. There were reconnections made, to my childhood self at the shattered frieze of Stac Pollaidh and at Achmelvich above all; to AK and MacCaig at Inverkirkaig and the pools of the Kirkaig river where his mind returned so often towards the end of his life. To Achiltibuie and the Summer Isles, unwitting objects of my first song. To Clachtoll and Stoer, where in the silence of sea-pinks, dried seaweed and straggly sheep, my father had first talked about the Highland Clearances.

I saw small groups of scattered houses, the odd isolated one, a few new builds. I noticed the grassed-over rickles of stones that had once been homes, and the darker lines near the shore that had been lazy-beds. They were kin to the moraine drumlins, also left by great retreats.

I saw very few people. I saw great emptiness. Forty-eight townships had been cleared in this parish alone. Hard to imagine thousands of people had once lived in Assynt. I would later be told by Mark Lazzarie, development manager at the recently bought-back Glencanisp Estate, that the estate's population had gone from some 1,800 in the mid-nineteenth century to . . . 2.

Heading back along Loch Assynt, my eyes went to the

ruins of Ardvreck castle out on its promontory. It had been a stronghold of the MacLeods of Assynt until they were dispossessed by the Mackenzies. And this more substantial ruin by the lochside was Calda House, which ruined the Mackenzie chief who built it. I got out and walked around Calda, thinking it was not that big, just two stories and an attic, no larger than any Lowland country house. Even at the top end, these people were never that wealthy.

I stood at the gable end, my hand on old stone, looking at the land on both sides of that long, glittering loch. So empty, so beautiful. So wrong.

> *Who owns this landscape? –*
> *The millionaire who bought it or*
> *the poacher staggering downhill in the early morning*
> *with a deer on his back?*

To people who live here, these are Norman MacCaig's best-known and most treasured lines, cropping up again and again in people's memories, in articles, pamphlets, guide books, school lessons and histories of the North West Highlands.

When 'A man in Assynt' came up in conversation, Norman's eyes would swivel off sideways then return. He'd make a slight grimace, that trout-like pout. 'Not a very good poem,' he said to me once. I had the sense not to agree aloud.

He was right, I think. There are memorable passages, particularly the opening and the closing, but in between either rather heavy-handed didacticism or chopped-up discursive prose can take over. At times it reads like bad MacDiarmid. It never reaches the heights nor the unity of his friend Sorley MacLean's transcendent laments like 'Hallaig'. The result of a rare commission, 'A man in Assynt' is both his longest and his only openly politically committed work. Neither suits his innate scepticism and talent for epigram and short lyric.

But though he had doubts about the poem's quality, I never heard him voice doubt about its central thrust. Much as he rejoiced in the people and landscape he loved best, he was also saddened and angered by their past and present circumstances.

To would-be revolutionaries, the crofters' apparent acceptance of their position could be exasperating. They opted for the comforts of wry humour, conviviality and whisky, plus – at least for Free Presbyterians – the certainty that Lord Vestey would burn in Hell for all Eternity, not being among the Elect or having the Gaelic. And there was always poaching, which was in part an economic necessity and, in the hands of a master like AK MacLeod, also an entertaining expression of the way things really are. AK was that man staggering downhill with a deer on his back or trout inside his jacket, and many loved him for it.

> *Who possesses this landscape? –*
> *The man who bought it or*
> *I who am possessed by it?*

Where does it come from, the centuries-old sense of injustice, betrayal, loss and dispossession that hangs over the Gaeltachd still, like whiffs of mustard gas haunting the trenches long after the war has moved elsewhere?

In our Lowland schools we were taught about Culloden and the Clearances – the former presented as a tragic and humiliating English victory over Scotland, the latter as its consequence. I now know both of these are misleading. Our version of Culloden omitted to mention that more Lowland Scots than English soldiers fought against the Highlanders that day.

Though Culloden was a defining tragedy for Gaeldom, it was not for the rest of Scotland. The peace, assured stability and prosperity that followed in Lowland Scotland were a precondition for the Scottish Enlightenment, perhaps the one aspect of my country's history of which I am unequivocally proud. Had Charles Edward Stuart won the day, there would have been no Hutton, Hume, Robertson or Black, Adam Smith or Watt, Playfair or Napier.

There is a loop back to James Hutton. As the Jacobite army approached an undefended Edinburgh (both the English garrison and the town council having hastily left the premises), a local defence force was set up. 'The College Company of Volunteers' was centred upon Colin Maclaurin, disciple of Newton, one of the most brilliant young mathematicians in Europe, and eighteen-year-old James Hutton's professor at the University. The scholars' attempts to rebuild the city's defences were assisted by a seventeen-year-old

Robert Adam, who would become the definitive Georgian architect.

This improbable grouping of professors, students, elderly folk and country people – a sort of Dad's Army – melted away when the Jacobites entered the city by an unsecured gate. But it expressed the typical Lowland reaction. To the students, clerics, merchants, academics, the Jacobites were not romantic revolutionaries but embarrassing, threatening anachronisms. Nor did the Lowland poor embrace them, for they saw no prospect of improvement from a foreign-tongued army whose ranks were even poorer than they were.

The last thing the Protestant, non-Gaelic speaking, non-clannish, hard-headed, practical, empirical and increasingly prosperous people of the Lowlands wanted was to see the high-handed Catholic Stuart kings restored. The Lowland Scottish regiments had no problems with joining the force that would harry the Highlanders homewards till they finally met on a plateau of poor pasture and heath, south of Inverness.

Culloden battlefield remains a dreary, despairing, brutal place. But the roots of the Clearances go much further back, all the way to the fall of the Lordship of the Isles nearly three hundred years earlier.

The Norse–Gaelic Clan Donald, whose power lay in the galley and the sword, had held sway for generations in the Western Isles and much of the seaboard, Kintyre, Assynt, Skye, Ardnamurchan, Wester and Easter Ross. These days their enemies would call them war lords, but their unifying rule was in many ways a golden age of the Gaeltachd.

I am haunted by a phrase from a Gaelic lament Sorley MacLean once quoted to me: *Ni h-eibhneas gan Chlainn Domhnaill.* 'There is no joy without Clan Donald.' When Sorley said it, the sound was desolate wind on an empty shoreline.

The Lords of the Isles' downfall came when John MacDonald made a treaty with Edward IV of England. He was stripped of most of his lands, and in 1476 the Lordship was taken into the hands of the Scottish Crown.

This was soon followed by a hundred years of mayhem, blood-letting, uprisings, slaughters and jostling for power throughout the Highlands and Islands as clan kinship unravelled. This anarchy and disruption became intolerable to the Scottish Crown, and James VI and I finally imposed the Statutes of Iona in 1609 – for the Gaeltachd, an event as significant as the '45 and the Clearances, for it led directly to both.

These Statutes systematically undermined the independence, and the very nature, of clan structure. The carrying of arms was outlawed, as were the firebrand Gaelic bards, the bearers of memory, singers of who the people are. The foundation of Presbyterian churches was enforced, as was the setting-up of parochial schools that were profoundly hostile to the Gaelic language and would not teach in it. The eldest son of a chief must be sent south for education. The chiefs also lost their right of heritable jurisdiction – to be lawgivers and arbiters of disputes, one of their key roles.

Under these and other pressures the social structures, the understanding of the relation between land, chief and clansman disintegrated. Well before the '45, the shift towards the commodification of land – a process as ugly as the word – was established. Absentee landlordism, forced relocation, rent-raising, mortgaging, all took a grip. Culloden accelerated that process.

The destructiveness of the imposed Statutes of Iona makes the clans support of the Stuart kings one of our history's painful ironies. It may also explain why a good number of clan chiefs did not come out for Charles Edward Stuart.

In the old understanding, the chief represented the clan, led it in battle, was the final lawgiver. He owed loyalty and honour to his kinsmen, as they owed it to him. He did not in any way own their livelihood, their homes or their land.

The clan system was not perfect – feuds, blood-lettings, brutal massacres and betrayals were common enough. Land was, in the end, won and held by force of arms, the sword rather than the lawyer and accountant's pen. Yet the shift from the old system – a world view, a shared understanding of the nature and identity of people, kinship, history and place – to a new commercialism where the people and their land and its use became commodities, is an event as tragic and painful as the one that can be glimpsed through the steady smirr of rain falling on the mute mounds and hollows of Culloden.

In an erosion as irresistible as any observed by James

Hutton, the clan chiefs shifted from a notion of leadership to one of ownership. Rents could be raised to meet their financial needs, people could be cleared off the land for the more profitable sheep, and later for deer. Estates could be sold, borrowed against, or owned from afar.

The glens and islands drained of people, who moved – sometimes through force, often because there was no better alternative – to the growing cities, or to the New World. Through the nineteenth century, the exit trickle became a flood, as though someone had pulled the plug from the green bath of the glens. Those who stayed were forcibly relocated to the coastal fringes, to land unsuitable for sheep or deer. They moved to croft the tiny, beautiful, scattered 'townships' of Stoer, Clathtoll, Clashnessie, Achmelvich, Drumbeg, Achnacarnin and Balchladich, names impossible to sound without feeling the poetry and the loss.

Defeated militarily, abandoned or betrayed by their leaders, baffled by the loss of an unspoken tradition that constituted their world, all that was left for the people were sorrowful songs, poverty and unremitting work with no prospect of improvement, emigration, whisky with a side-dish of poaching, and the strange consolation of extreme Calvinism in the schismatic sects of the Presbyterian Church.

And you wonder why, though the West moves me in ways no other part of the world can, I don't live there?

The people who remained never forgot. Gaelic-speaking or not – and little native Gaelic remains in Assynt – that culture is intensely oral, obsessed with genealogy and family story. For them this is much more than nostalgia. Family, kinship and place of residence constitute who you are, what can be expected of you.

When Norman introduced me to Sorley MacLean, last of the high Gaelic bards, a singer of his people's songs who would have been proscribed by the Statutes of Iona, the one who hauled Gaelic poetry into political modernity, the very first thing Sorley said to me was 'And who are your people?'

Not 'How are you?' or 'What do you do?' While Norman looked on amused, I explained my father's family were from Arbroath on the east coast, not part of the clan system, and my mother was from Northumberland.

'Yes, but who *are* your people?'

I told him I'd never met my paternal grandparents or any of my uncles – they'd all emigrated and died – or indeed any relative of my father, and I wasn't even very sure of their names, had no idea what they'd done or where they'd lived or who their descendants were, so I really, really had no people on my father's side.

He looked at me, baffled, shocked, then shook his head. That head, so splendidly vague in many daily matters, contained many thousands of detailed genealogical linkages, connections to precise places, histories, individuals and events that laid a web of meaning and identity over his native Raasay, Skye, most of the Western Isles and seaboard, and much of the Western Highlands.

I later saw him several times, on first meeting a fellow

Gael, exchange names, places, occupations, physiognomies, dates, until he finally established to his own satisfaction who that person's people were. Then he could relax. Then he knew who that person was. Sorley had that memory and cast of mind to an extraordinary degree, but it was highly typical of his culture.

And me, for the first time I felt bereft. Back then I had brothers and a sister, mother and father, but I did not have a people.

To Norman the Assynt Crofters' Buy-Out, concluded in February 1993 when the crofters purchased the North Lochinver Estate from the administrators of a bankrupt Swedish property company, was a matter of deep satisfaction at the end of his life.

The news of that improbable buy-out ran like a beneficent shock-wave across the Highlands and Islands of Scotland. It was the first sign of reversal of hundreds of years of betrayal, loss and decline, and went on to trigger many others. Its significance went way beyond a legal transfer. From start to finish, the buy-out was profoundly an emotional event, and succeeded because it harnessed that emotion, and that emotion sourced in history, surely as the Kirkaig river rushing into the bay sources in the dubs, burns and bogs that lie between Suilven and Cul Mor.

It was led by three particularly passionate, imaginative and able people: John MacKenzie, Allan Macrae and Bill Ritchie, respectively the vice chairman, the chairman and treasurer of the Assynt branch of the Scottish Crofters Union.

In the past, estates in the Highlands and Islands had been occasionally offered for purchase, but the crofters had not taken up the opportunity. Experience and disappointment had taught them caution and stoicism, a kind of innate conservatism. A croft has been well described as a small piece of land surrounded by acres of legislation. They had their security of tenure, low rents and low incomes; they didn't look or hope for much. If the landowner or their factor were tolerable, why change things? Is it not wiser – and simply easier – to shrug, mourn the ancient loss, have a dram and enjoy what is there to be enjoyed?

But this time was different. The North Lochinver Estate had been bought by the Vestey family from a Mr Filmer-Sankey, who had been given it as a wedding present by the Duke of Westminster. (If you made this up, it would seem heavy-handed satire.) It was later sold to a Swedish property company. Naturally the crofters were not consulted. Three years later that company went bankrupt and the liquidator put up the estate for sale in seven lots.

At this point the Assynt crofters became seriously alarmed. This proposed fragmentation threatened to damage and entangle their daily lives. The familiar notion of a crofting community within a large estate would be replaced by small commercial lots, a final atomisation of the old ways.

This anxiety was fuelled into anger by the sale particulars, which stressed the estate's wonderful qualities of 'wilderness', emptiness, silence and wildlife. That people actually lived and worked there was glossed over, as were the 172 crofts with their complex rights; they were not what the estate was about. It was about the rare and wondrous quality of emptiness.

Led by able, eloquent and organised people, the North Lochinver Estate crofters determined to buy the estate as a whole. After a whirlwind campaign of seven months, full of bids, counter-bids, bluffs, public meetings, public appeals, working the quangos (people became accustomed to an acronym broth of HRC, HIE, CASE, SNA) and inspired media encounters, on 8th December 1992 they finally succeeded.

It was and remains a historic, landmark moment in the history of the Scottish Highlands and Islands. They won against the odds and precedents because they were united. Because they grasped the importance of media coverage in not merely following but actually augmenting their campaign. (Parts of the Scottish media became allies and advisers of the steering committee.) They won because of widespread public support across the Gaeltachd, across Scotland, with donations coming from New Zealand, Canada, USA. The local MP, Robert Maclennan, hardly a dangerous radical, made a significant donation to the purchase fund, and spoke with feeling of the clearance of his fore-bears. They won because not only were they in the right, but their strategies were smart. They used their heads as well as their hearts.

Strategy, canniness, working the quangos, ensuring good PR, fund-raising are all important. But I think the reason why in the end – almost to their own astonishment – they succeeded was epitomised in John MacKenzie's response to an interviewer from *The Independent* when she asked why it was so important they owned the land. He pointed at the lines of stones outside his house at Culkein Drumbeg. These were mute remains of the work his forebears, his people, had put in on this stony, rough, poor land. They had been cleared in 1819 from Inchnadamph to Canisp, and moved on again to this place. *That* was why it mattered.

Sometimes a story is not just a story. Sometimes it can move not mountains, but the ownership of them. Which is of course, as MacCaig observed, ridiculous. We own nothing in this world, mountains, rivers and lochs least of all.

The celebratory ceilidh at the Culag Hotel in Lochinver is still talked about. 'Oh, it was a fine evening,' one discreet woman said to me. 'A right damn wild hoolie!' a well-oiled friend enthused. But whatever they say, and whatever the problems that follow from taking back responsibility for one's own life – and there have been unintended consequences, disappointments and bad feeling, along with the rejuvenation – their eyes glow as Norman's did, remembering.

> *And the mind*
> *behind the eye, within the passion,*
> *remembers with certainty that the tide will return*
> *and thinks, with hope, that that other ebb,*
> *that sad withdrawal of people, may, too,*
> *reverse itself and flood*
> *the bays and the sheltered glens*

with new generations replenishing the land
with its richest of riches and coming, at last,
into their own again.

Retrieve: the competitive novel

'Fifteen to thirteen!' Andy exclaimed happily as he slung his wet pack in the car. 'Great day! So glad I'm not in New York.'

I looked to Peter. 'Mostly small ones,' he said. 'It's rice and dall for tea tonight.'

I turned the car round and we headed off back to base camp.

'Good day, Greigy?'

'Yes,' I replied. 'Feels like I covered a lot of ground.'

The low sun dropped out of cloud, and we sat on the shingle watching saffron being scattered in long blurry furrows on the loch. We'd been silent for a while, all thought displaced by hill, water, light, sky.

'We've dreamed up a ploy for a competitive novel,' Andy announced. 'It starts from a trip we made as students, and something that happened to a pal.'

'What's the competition?' I enquired.

'Who writes it first,' Peter said, thoughtfully stirring the dall. He stayed like that, abstracted yet listening intently, tending the stove and our evening meal, as his brother told me about his Dutch friend Siete.

In Bologna on the second of August 1980, Siete had left his friends on the train station platform while he went to get bread and wine. The terrorist bomb went off as he came back up the station steps. Inside, his friends and eighty-three others were dead. He saw it all.

I vaguely remembered the Bologna bombing. Around that time I'd spent an evening with a Glaswegian who said he was looking to join the Provos. Only violence could expose the State's violent oppression of Ulster, only armed struggle could reverse it. He rolled joints, played songs on the guitar (badly). His rage was real. I left not entirely sure he was a fantasist.

'Who did it?' I asked.

'At the time it was said to be Red Brigade,' Peter said. 'Now they think it was far right Nationalists, maybe with help from a Masonic order and elements in the security service. Or maybe not. It's Italian, it gets very complicated.'

'But that's not what the novel would really be about,' Andy said. 'Not the bombing itself, or pretending we can get inside those minds. It would be more about the consequences for the people still alive.'

I rolled on my side and stared at the fuzzy low sun across the loch as Andy talked of how after many years of believing the event had not affected him deeply, Siete had abruptly entered a prolonged breakdown, and on emerging remade his life from a work-focused, fast-living, uptight cosmopolitan publisher, to living in a hut with his occasional girlfriend, happy, poor, relaxed.

In the course of this 'exorcism' he had also acquired a heated healing touch that could soothe headaches, ease pains, unknot muscles. He was slightly scared of it, in truth, and only used it sparingly, for friends and relatives in pain or anguish. He hoped it would stay with him, as some-thing gained from the trauma. Last time they had met, he said *Andrew, no man can die more than once.*

In the silence by the lochside after he finished, each of us took Andy's story in his own way. For Andy I think it was a story about trauma, denial, then changing one's way of life. If the life of focused, high-income, demanding work was in some way false, where did that leave him?

For myself, I wondered if I was still in a post-traumatic phase. Certainly I had no new powers, no heated hands. I just had an acute awareness of the mortality of everyone I met. Even our Metaphysical Policeman, so canny and alert, was nearly dead even as he walked towards us. You look in someone's eyes, see the infant, the child, the teenager and the middle-aged adult, the old person, the corpse that dwells in there.

On bad days, indifference; in bad moments, terror; in good hours, beauty and compassion. I sipped the last of my whisky. That sense of our powerlessness was as near to a new power as I was likely to get.

And Peter? He served up the dall and said little, but I learned later he was thinking of the would-be existential drifter musician that had been part of him in his teens. Who lurked there still, within the doctor and family man in his late thirties. Who demanded recognition, resurrec-tion, reconciliation before a more candid parting of the ways.

He would later write the 'competitive novel' conceived of on that Assynt trip, at a time when terrorism was something located in the past. It would be called *Nightingale* after the sleazy bohemian café-bar in Bologna where a young Scottish musician becomes drawn into a crowd of wasters, lovers, idealists and fantasists. There would be a woman, of course, and behind her someone who was definitely not a fantasist. These ingredients were stirred in the pot with added spices and fresh ingredients, then stirred around the blackened, battered saucepan of the inner life, until ready to serve.

'This is great, Ned!' Andy slurped. 'Really good.'

And so it was.

Cast: at the end of the day

I would never say my father was a cold man. He was hot, a heat that sometimes flared in irritation, anger and impatience. Men of that generation were built for endurance and dignity, but few were for joy, curiosity or spontaneity. They wore hats or flat bonnets depending on class, and nearly all wore ties, even at home – and they kept much under their hat, and so much of what they could have said was caught at the throat.

That kind of dignity – MacCaig had it too – has largely vanished from these islands. It was impressive and honourable. Yet their dignity stemmed from opacity, their strength from their reticence, their endurance from some inner hardening. Too often those men were not emotionally available to their children, their friends, their spouse, even as their own parents had not been available to them.

If that constraint, that harshness, that self-limitation is masculinity, they can keep it. Years ago I rejected much my father stood for, yet now I feel him run through me like Hutton's veins of granite intruded through softer rock. Without my version of his stubborn drive, the thrawn resilience that took him through two world wars, his bloody-mindedness, I doubt if I'd be here today. I'd have given up, settled for less, kept writing as my hobby, never risked my neck on big hills.

Sensitivity is not enough. You need some igneous stuff,

some old material metamorphosed, and some upthrust, otherwise life just erodes you.

In the absence of the women at the centre of our lives, for those days in Assynt we could in some way *relax*. Though the Dorward boys kept up high standards of personal hygiene, bathing naked in the loch each morning, without women to keep us on our toes we let certain other standards drop. Shorn of the status-wrestling that so often seems to pass for friendship among men, we could just fish, walk, eat, talk, read. Our intimacy was in what we didn't need to discuss, in the casual chat as much as the personal, the kinds of silences there could be between us. Above all, it was in the shared doing.

The yarns, the dangling conversations, and the solitary time fishing or climbing into the hills or lying in the tent, that was when we ripened inside. The past had time to become present again; the present had time to be reflected on. That third day in Assynt, with its mixed weathers, was not a wasted one.

To catch up with your own life (and your culture's past) is basic hygiene, not nostalgia or indulgence. *The unexamined life is not worth living.* I agree, and at that point part company with my father and a certain version of being a man. But I honour his endurance, his strength, his application and unexpected moments of humour and affection, and see no reason to chuck them out among the rubble of this quarrying.

I see now that on this trip we were offering each other

stories. Stories that subtly altered the teller, and that the listeners drew into themselves to be altered in turn. When we told stories of friends, illnesses, losses, encounters, farcical failure and muddled success, we were entertaining each other but also provoking those tiny internal reconfigurations by which we may catch up with where we are now.

You catch up with your life or, like Siete vomiting uncontrollably by the roadside on the Brenner Pass, it catches up with you.

The ground was soggy after rain, and to minimise the midges that thrived in the damp vegetation, after eating we moved the tents down onto the shingle beach. Peter poured wine into our mugs then laid the empty bottle on the shingle. We needed to buy more supplies soon, or catch our fish and be gone. Like MacCaig's summers, our time here was purchased by work we had done elsewhere.

We agreed that tomorrow, whatever the weather, we would climb back up to the Green Corrie and put in a full day there.

We passed round the chocolate and entertained ourselves with quoting from John Berryman's *Dream Songs*. Although it was at the other end of the poetic spectrum from MacCaig, for years Andy and I had loved that wild demotic, the mangled syntax, outrageous personal confession mixed with fiction and fragments of planet news. An American voice, unreined and expansive, so far from Norman's canny, ironic clarity.

Poetry is the most portable of art forms, carried in

completeness in the mind. After a concluding and unarguable *Aye, in Sealdah station some possessionless children survive to die* we fell silent and watched the lowering sun expand into a misshapen red blob, then wobble into the sea. There was no green ray at its disappearing. Tonight the sunset sky was muted, as we were, laid-back gradations of saffron, pink, glowing grey.

When that was done, we scoured the plates with gravel and heather, washed our faces in the loch, brushed our teeth and went to our tents. For a while the other torches moved, then went out. I finished my notes then lay looking at the orange fabric lift and drop, as though the tent were breathing.

The first night Lesley and I spent together, I lay awake as long as possible watching her sleep in the lamplight. I tried to commit her face to memory. When we fall in love, a truly smart bomb has gone off, one that brings people back to life and obliterates all we thought we owned.

What happens next is inevitable only in fairy tales. We don't know where we're going. We are still waiting to see what turns up.

I thought of the dub, those green reed aerials quivering. My palm remembered the rough damp of the Knockan Crag where I had stroked the surface of Deep Time. I saw Norman, staring patiently ahead as I fitted his hearing aid.

I held a face up before me like a lantern in the gloaming, said her name aloud, then let go.

Retrieve: a little night vision

It was as though someone had dropped a shilling in one of those now-defunct telescopes mounted at outlook points on promenades of decaying last resorts. The darkness clicked open. I was looking at a very distant scene and a friend, brought close-up.

When I left my wife I was poor as I deserved to be. Income, furniture, surroundings, all reverted back towards student life. It was what I'd wanted. I had a lover, the one whom years later I would finally let go of in the Pentland Hills. I was homeless, shaky and thin-skinned.

Don Coppock held the lease on a shabby ground-floor flat on Thirlestane Road, Edinburgh. He was American, a few years younger than me, tall, muscular, with short brown hair and neat moustache. He wore new jeans and checked shirts, had the complexion of someone who spent a lot of time outdoors and looked after himself. His handshake was strong as he accepted me into the flat.

In his quiet way, Don was determined to spread the message. He would go away weekends with friends to talk at meetings, go on demos, and hand out Gay Rights leaflets on the streets of Glasgow, Perth, Dundee, Inverness.

'Balls of steel, Andy,' he grinned when I admired his nerve. 'Besides, it gets me out of the house and onto your fantastic hills.'

He had to explain to me who John Muir was. He couldn't

believe I had never heard of the Dunbar-born Scot who became the founder, the icon of Nature Conservation in North America. Don spent his summer vacations working on projects with the Sierra Club and the John Muir Trust in Yosemite, the place Muir explored, wrote about, spent many solitary times in, and managed to lobby to save from extinction under logging and damming.

A lot of lively young men came calling at that flat. Most would sum me up in a glance and dismiss me as not part of the cause and the fun. But Don always had time to listen to my difficulties and would talk openly about his own, with family, parents, sister, boyfriends. He didn't care that I was straight. I appreciated that.

'Straight or gay, Andy, it's the same old same old. Except we have to fight for our rights and you don't.'

He didn't feel sorry for himself. He was pissed off and frustrated that people could be so dumb, and he was still trying to heal things with his family, but he didn't see himself as hard done by. He was warm, funny, rueful, open-minded and curious. He was my first and I think best gay friend.

Eventually Don moved back to California. A year or two later I went to stay with him in San Francisco. Impossible to remember now how I came to be in North America, but it must have involved a writing residency or a festival or a woman. Writing, and the need for money and emotional rescue, drove me through that low decade.

I got off a trolley bus, asked directions and walked towards the sea. At the end of the block the beach stretched in sun and haze, and beyond that waves broke. The Pacific Ocean. It was autumn and the beach was near-empty. Alone on the sand sat a gutted television set. Ah, California!

Don had a small house on a sloping street. He came to the door in new blue jeans, check shirt and trail boots. He took me to meet his 'main boyfriend', Larry, who lived round the corner. Larry was wearing an Oriental dressing gown and seemed to have modelled himself on Noel Coward as he made spritzers. He hadn't been very well for a while, and only got dressed to go out.

Don and I walked downtown, into a quarter where I was very much a minority. 'It's all gotten very political,' Don explained. He pointed out some bars he wouldn't advise us going in – people would suss me out straight away and might be offended at my presence. 'Sorry about that,' he said. 'Things are a bit overheated right now.'

He did take me into a coffee house called Kiss My Sweet, buzzing with chat, caffeine, camp and sugar-rush. 'This is my friend Andy from Scotland. He's straight.'

'Live and let live, I say,' one mate of Don's commented. Outside, the streets, bars, sidewalks were buzzing with some kind of contact high. A constant parade of performance, all the clichés of leather jackets and peaked caps, lumberjacks, queens, transvestites, meeting and greeting and parting like bees, urgently carrying secret pollen from one source to another. I could see why Don had left Edinburgh.

I asked about the 'main boyfriend'. Don explained in the gay community many felt it was time to stop aping the straight world with its coupledom and ideal of lifelong commitments. There was sex. A *lot* of sex. Which was great, he affirmed, only sometimes it all seemed a bit heartless. 'Maybe I'm just a romantic, Andy.' He was worried about Larry.

We drove inland, through endless orange groves, to the mountains and Yosemite. For two days we walked trails there, Don talking and enthusing about John Muir, the new conservation movement, its struggles with the Republican administration, the work he was doing leading volunteers. The air smelled like chilled retsina.

We came out of the trees onto the top of the waterfall dropping hundreds of feet – I remember that falling-away, and how it felt inside. Later, a brown bear and cub, met suddenly at twilight, ten yards away. Don whispered we couldn't outrun it, and bears can climb trees better than we can. We stood motionless, trying to make ourselves supremely unthreatening. The world became that big head turning, turning in the dimness for a long time before bear and cub abruptly tanked into the undergrowth.

Chill at nights, the air pine-filled. We slept in a lamp-lit damp cabin by a river, me in the bunk by the window because I've always needed an out. We talked of affairs of the heart, family, the wonder and awfulness of the world, Scotland and California. He told me about his first girl-friend and the long journey from then on.

All gay people have made that journey against the current. Wild salmon do it, that's where their muscle comes from. In that respect, I go with the current. I have not had that clearly defined struggle to recognise myself, then assert my right to be so. Maybe the breakdown and divorce, that falling-out of the world anticipated for me, the anxious or angry friends and family, was as near as I'd come to an act of self-definition. Or building my life around the writing of poetry, accepting the absence of money, stability and career.

Whenever I hear that story of early days that all gay people can tell – the self-knowledge, the struggle, the cost – I feel inadequate and not a little envious. Carried along by the main current, how can I know I want to go where it is taking me?

'Goodnight, Andy.'

'Night, Don.'

Lamp turned down and blown out. We lay in the darkness listening to the water. Wind in trees and owls hooting. Lost, lost, born off downstream to wherever.

Months later, Don wrote to say Larry was very ill. It had a name now: AIDS. Then Larry died. That whole glittering, buzzing scene died. When people wrote hateful things about God's punishment or self-inflicted disaster, I pictured Larry shuffling round the house in his silk dressing gown, pouring white wine, and the jubilant hive clustered round the goodies at Kiss My Sweet. I feared for Don.

In time he wrote to say he was now HIV positive. Then another couple of years on the new drugs before he developed AIDS. He wrote he had always wanted to lose weight but had never thought it would be down the toilet. Then of course he died too.

His sister sent me the news and enclosed a copy of a late entry from Don's journal, an account of a lucid dream he had had of dancing with animals. Out in his beloved wilderness, scared at first then jubilant and dancing naked with the animals in the light of a great fire, full of vigour, restored, whole, at one with them. He wrote that since that dream he was not scared of dying.

Lying in my tent in deepest Assynt, sighting down the barrel of years, I think of him. A brave man, good friend, lover of the natural world. My throat thickens. Our own mortality is one thing; that of others, quite another.

He would have enjoyed this quest. Tomorrow I will cast for Don, and as I send my line out over the water, think of him dancing with the animals, exultant and unafraid.

Time was up, the shutter clicked down, I slept again.

DAY 4

Cast: the right size of hill

I woke into a bright, hot orange world. I spread my hand
and felt shingle through the groundsheet, heard the stove
hiss. My tent flap unzipped.

'Tea, Greigy?'

A weathered hand pushed a red mug in my direction.
For a moment I was at Base Camp on the Lhotse Shar
expedition, sirdar Dawa passing in the morning brew to
wash away altitude headache.

I sat up in my bag, drinking and letting the new day in.
These vivid returns of lovers and friends, by night and in
broad daylight – something was going on. Ground was
being cleared, though too soon to say for what. My inner
life seems to operate on a need-to-know basis.

I drained the tea and stuck my head out into the dazzle.
Zillions of tiny suns bounced in the distant sea round the
islands. Quinag sprawled in its monumental totality. Light
breeze from the north twirled long grass by the loch. I
wanted it all so much it almost hurt.

Hunkered by the stove, scoffing porridge, Andy grinned
and stretched.

'Today is the day!'

It always is, though some days more so than others.

Today we did not rush straight up the steep ground behind
our camp. Instead we took the path along the shore then

207

turned uphill, following a good-sized burn. At first, full of bright energy, we were talking away, about memories of MacCaig, pantheism, geology, the prospects for Scottish rugby this autumn, and the curious indifference of our English friends and partners to being English. Then the gradient began to separate us out, and we saved our breath.

Lichen-spattered Lewisian gneiss boulders, steep stony path where flakes of mica glinted. Crystals of quartzite, white and pink, washed down from the tops. The tumble of water cooling and moistening the air, the smell of earth and heather as the sun grew higher, the ache in upper thighs, that was our world for a while.

We gained the bealach and pulled off our fleece jackets. We looked across the glen to Quinag, then out to the sunlit islands in Eddrachillis Bay. Tiny frogs rustled again at our feet, and we thought of AK and Norman and Norman MacAskill, who must have stood here on mornings like this. Others would stand here again when we were gone, and still know it beautiful.

We agreed we love our country's hills in part for being *the right size*. Big enough to make significant demands, yet small enough to walk over, to know and feel connected to. There is no mountain in Scotland you cannot walk up and back down in a day, though that day might be long and the hill can be fatal. There is not a lochan or burn or top or bealach or corrie here that does not have a name, a story, that does not live in someone's memory. The Lake District, even the Welsh hills, the Peak District, are all fine and bonnie, but a little . . . domestic. The Himalayas were awesome, astounding, possibly sublime, but I did not come to love them. They were too big to love; love implies some possible knowledge.

But Suilven, Cul Mor, Canisp, Quinag, Glas Bheinn, are just the size to possess us. They rise above the human, without being entirely beyond us.

Peter quoted a remark by the social historian James Hunter, to the effect that the typical empty Highland glen was no more natural than a railway embankment. We concurred that in the end instead of this stunning emptiness we would rather see lights on in the glen, deer-fences and the natural reforestation that would follow, and signs of human occupation.

Yet as we spoke I was looking across the glaciated valley at the immense corries and ridge-lines of Quinag. Fact remains that the uppermost slopes and tops of these Assynt hills are uninhabitable, up where even heather and thin turf give out, leaving only bare rock.

The bald dome of Suilven, the fretted castellation of Stac Pollaidh, the implacable Cuillin Ridge – the whole of the Highlands would have looked like this when the last glaciers retreated, before vegetation and then people moved back in: scoured rock, rubble and water. These heights are innately wild and untouchable, and I love that too, for there is no question of our settling there or having any real impact. Only another ice age can significantly alter them. Only the buzzard drifts over.

On one level, namely ours, Assynt is profoundly human. It exists in and through human labour, memory, story, naming;

it is resurrected complete and entire in Norman's poems. The buy-outs, the taking back of the land, and the energies and hope that unleashes, might indeed bring back lights to the glens. But still these highest tops will rise beyond us; we can never occupy them, and they remain embodiments of processes and realities that make our Clearances, our Global Warming, seem puny.

They put us in our place, and that is healing.

'Enough blethering,' Andy said. 'We've got fish to catch!'

The unacknowledged rest over, we pressed on over the rough ground, up into the dyke swarms, dubs, outcrops and buttresses that conceal the Loch of the Green Corrie. Human into the non-human, with sweat our connection to the world, we felt ourselves the right size.

Retrieve: an unfair question

As we approached Loch Bealach a Bhuirich where a chilly
mist still lurked, Peter said 'Do you mind if I try a spot of
fishing here?' Andy hesitated then opted to go on, and my
focus had always been on the Green Corrie. So we left
Peter there, checked the map and pressed on up.

As we climbed I told Andy how I went to see Norman
when he had just published his last collection, *Voice-Over*.
I'd bought the book that afternoon, only had time for a
quick read through it. As soon as I was sat down and given
a dram, he'd quizzed me.

'So, have you read it?'

'Yes, but only very quickly.'

He waved his hand. 'Quick is good enough.' He paused,
drew on his tube of fresh air and looked at me. 'So tell me
– what is the best poem in the book?'

'Norman, you can't ask that!'

He giggled. 'I know. But what *is* the best poem?'

I could only spread my hands and tell the truth.

'The one that stood out was "On the pier at Kinlochbervie".'

'You're right!' I see still his look. Pride at something well
done. Pleasure that the quality of that stripped and desperate
poem was evident to another. Glee at being naughty enough
to solicit. He stubbed out his cigarette and lit another, leaned
back in his chair. 'Now tell me – what is the second-best
poem in the book?'

After I'd refused to play that game any further, he confessed that for a long time after Isabel's death he had written nothing. She had suffered so much, poetry seemed puny.

'So I miss that too.'

Nothing I could say to that. He lowered his long, patrician nose into his glass, sniffed. 'My children and grandchildren are very good to me, otherwise I'd be a lonely old codger. Yet I've been a lucky fellow all my days . . . I suppose I should feel guilty about that.' Pause, roll of eyes, flashing grin. 'I don't in the least!'

In that little flash of defiance I glimpsed again Norman in his pomp. At the Poetry '71 Festival I'd spotted him, upright and elegant across a crowded, smoke-filled hospitality room in the David Hume Tower. Tall among his friends, glass in one hand, cigarette in the other, listening and alert as a heron, his plume of grey hair rising from that Greek philosopher's profile, with Goodsir Smith at his right setting the company in a roar and MacDiarmid fizzing to his left, and himself about to utter the remark that would not so much end the discussion as spin it off with a new glister to it – let me remember him like that, with his biggest losses and his best work still to come.

And that 'best poem' from his last collection? Andy and I spoke it aloud as we climbed, filling in each other's blank spots, as friends do.

On the pier at Kinlochbervie

The stars go out one by one
as though a bluetit the size of the world
were pecking them like peanuts out of the sky's
    string bag.

A ludicrous image, I know.

Take away the grey light.
I want the bronze shields of summer
or winter's scalding sleet.

My mind is struggling with itself.

That fishing boat is a secret
approaching me. It's a secret
coming out of another one.
I want to know the first one of all.

Everything's in the distance,
as I am. I wish I could flip that distance
like a cigarette into the water.

I want an extreme of nearness.
I want boundaries on my mind.
I want to feel the world like a straitjacket.

Norman MacCaig

Retrieve: playing Copsbrook

'On the pier at Kinlochbervie' is a classic instance of what Edward Said identified as 'Late Style', when works of radical directness, simplicity, complexity or oddity emerge. Think 'The Tempest', late Beethoven; late Yeats, late Cohen and Dylan.

'Late Style has the power to render disenchantment and pleasure without resolving the contradiction between them. What holds them in tension, as equal forces straining in opposite directions, is the artist's mature subjectivity, stripped of hubris and pomposity, unashamed either of its fallibility or the modest assurance it has gained . . .'

'Mature subjectivity', I like that. In Norman's case, we have poems that look so casual in structure, so simple and transparent, they are nearly invisible as poetry – until you let your lips move as you read.

Robert Frost – 'talking through a hole in his own practice', MacCaig remarked – said writing poetry without rhyme and metre was like playing tennis without a net. As if that were too easy. As if that were cheating.

In our early teens my brother Sandy and I evolved a site-specific game we called 'Copsbrook', after the villainous opposing team captain in the *Victor* boys' comic. We played it with a tennis ball on the concrete of our small backyard. One wall was the goal; the opposite wall was across a narrow flowerbed. To score a goal we had to complete a complex, satisfying, spontaneous series of passes – say foot to head to foot, foot then head, all aerial, then headed down to be slammed high into the wall with a joyful whoop.

Copsbrook did not exist. It was two of us against our own incompetence, for 'he' would score whenever a rebound or a mis-aimed pass went into the flowerbed behind us. And as for our score, it was a matter of our own judgement as to when the move was exciting, unexpected, complex and glorious enough to count for us. It had to bring delight, it had to be right. There was seldom argument or discussion needed; we knew in our hearts when it was good enough and when it was not.

We were the only players, only referee, only audience. The rules were invisible, unwritten, self-created. The game went on until it was finished, or we were. We played for hours, we played out this Manichean struggle between Good and Bad, Beauty and Ugliness, into lung-heaving exhaustion, and we often lost. When I was at university studying philosophy, at home we sometimes would resurrect Copsbrook, and the world would become real again.

Farcical, childish, absurd, too easy to play against a nonexistent competitor? MacCaig would have agreed with Eliot's remark 'There is no such thing as free verse.' I have never known a game as demanding, as absorbing, as pure and difficult as playing Copsbrook – unless it is trying to write a poem, a true poem, that has no visible constraints but bends around its inner necessity.

In his later poems, Norman managed it over and over. When he wrote 'On the pier at Kinlochbervie', he knew he had scored. The victorious gleam in his eye had its arms flung wide as Eric Cantona turning away from the goal, to share with the crowd the wonder he has just committed.

Cast: going up the outflow

After some wandering about in what geologists delight-
fully call a *dyke swarm*, we stumbled across an outflow burn
and followed it up. We climbed above the cloud that had
filled the glen below. It was hot and the insect world was
lively.

The burn gathered itself into pools, and familiar scree
slopes rose up. We hurried by the pools, over the rise, and
we were back again at the Lochan a Choire Ghuirm.

We may indeed get a person, place or situation at first
blink, but seeing them again tells us more. Three years earlier
I had hurried into Waverley station, uncertain what I would
see, and for a moment that neat figure in the crowded
concourse with the overnight bag and Sixties cap was smaller
and less significant than I'd remembered. Then I saw her
look around, a still point among the shifting crowd, so alert,
humane, wary, capable of joy, unique. Something opened
within as I walked towards one who had enriched my life
once, and would again.

I reread books and poems. I go back to the well and
draw the bucket up again. That's when you know. When I
see a poem or painting that does something to me, I go
away and come back to it later. Sometimes two returns are
enough. Sometimes you can see no end to possible returns.
Can two people live together for the rest of their lives
without exhausting each other?

'I'm beginning to see what MacCaig meant about this place,' Andy said.

We stood on our little promontory, assembling our rods. Today the lochan was two-toned, cornflower blue then gleaming platinum, with a sharp divide where the wind halted. Lewisian gneiss and quartzite scree, shimmering light overhead, in our ears the non-silence of wind and water.

It was an Assynt within Assynt, a small cradling, a stand-alone excerpt from a larger work.

On the first visit I'd valued this place because Norman had; on that hot midday return I began to value it for what it was. *Just H_2O in a hollow*, as MacCaig remarked of small lochs, *yet not much time passes without me thinking of them.* My lover's eyes were only pulpy, light-sensitive, glaucous nerve endings set in a hollow, yet not much time passed without me thinking of them.

'At the hospital they asked if I was your next of kin, and I realised of course I wasn't,' Lesley had said. Now I crouched in the Green Corrie and thought again of Sorley MacLean's question *Who are your people?*

I stood up, feeling slightly dizzy, trailed today's flies in the water to give them weight.

'Well, good luck,' Andy said, and set off. Then he stopped and turned. 'By the way, did MacCaig say what he thought was the second-best poem in *Voice-Over*?'

'"Between mountain and sea". You should have seen his face, like a wee boy dipping his fist into his personal sweetie jar.'

Andy strode confidently along the shore, sunny as the

cheerful fellow MacCaig claimed to be, and was, and wasn't. Swishing back and forward, I worked my line out then let it fly.

The casts seemed to be flowing better today. For the first time I truly began to believe this might work. I so wanted that fish for Norman. A slight tug and I twitched, took in the line. Nothing. Almost certainly a piece of weed, or just the chop on the water.

I cast out again. If you are uncertain whether you've had a bite or not, you haven't. I spent much of my thirties and forties in that state, wondering. When the real thing happens, there's no doubt. Except whether you will land it . . .

'Hey Greigy! Caught anything yet?'

Peter made me flinch, calling as he came up over the rise.

'We just got started. You?'

'No. Interesting loch, though.'

He seemed preoccupied and determined as he strode off down the left side of the lochan, rod in one hand, landing net in the other.

As he looked down into the water, trying to gauge what was going on in there, Peter brooded over what had happened down at the lower loch. He'd been fishing in the mist, getting chilly and damp but happy to be there, with cold hands and his thoughts moving over Andy's story about his friend who had missed being killed in the Bologna bombing. What had really been going on there? What if his friends weren't his friends? Perhaps he was *meant* to die there, but hadn't. In which case, the consequences . . .

As his thoughts ravelled, Peter had found himself watching a duck on its nest on a small island, being attacked by two large gulls. It stood up, flapped its wings, then shrank back over its nest as one gull then the other swooshed by. One gull landed in the water, made ready to land on the tiny island. The duck got up, hissed – and the other gull bombed down from above.

The duck got back onto its nest just in time. The first gull drifted at the edge of the island, waiting, its thuggish beak poised. The duck sat, its head turning nervously, trying to follow the attack from above and the one from the side.

This went on through thinning mist for ten minutes, quarter of an hour. As Peter fished, he could see that the duck could not keep it up. Sooner or later it would be driven off or be exhausted, then the eggs would be eaten in moments. Then the duck would fly away, failed in its biological imperative.

Worse – or was it better? – after feeling (in so far as a duck can) loss and regret for a few minutes or an hour or a day, it would then fly on, having forgotten all about it.

A grim vision of the way things are, one that would have satisfied the gloomy mind behind the new book he was reading. It felt right to Peter. Its spirit filtered into the inchoate novel he was imagining as he took in his line and set off uphill, leaving the duck and gulls to it.

It was with him still, stiffening his determination as he watched the surface of the Loch of the Green Corrie. Was that something there, close in, by that brown rock? He looked, twitched his forearm, directed the cast.

The book could be written. Fish would be caught today. The gulls will get the eggs.

Retrieve: the rings of Assynt

Andy took in his line and ambled back to me.

'Nothing. Maybe once this sun goes in – it's too bright right now.'

The wind had died on the water, the sun burned into the hollows winter had left round our eyes. A few midges were starting to take an interest.

'Lunch!' Andy called. Peter waved his free arm without taking his eyes off the water, cast twice more then joined us.

We lay at ease on the promontory, eating oatcakes and cheese, dates and flapjack. Musty tea from battered metal flasks. Slight ache in under the right shoulder. Idle chat between friends. There are times you taste being alive. Swallow it. Breathe it in and out, a presence like air itself, invisible and everywhere.

'Do you think,' Andy said, 'it would do someone some-where hellish any good if we weren't happy chappies now?'

The smoke from Andy's roll-up rose straight then dissipated, scattering the midges. I made a few notes, then just looked. Peter turned another page of W.G. Sebald's *The Rings of Saturn* – today's light reading – and chuckled.

'So depressing, so arcane! So true!'

He approved the unrelenting pessimism of Sebald's outlook. I'd found it fascinating, then irritating, then faintly hilarious. The man with the doleful moustache was the Eeyore of European intellectual history. There is a sly entertainment in a man who, on a coastal walk through Suffolk, can only see loss, decline, ancient crimes, collapse. He sees and remembers only sad, terrible things, and he encounters only grotesques, the lonely and the lost, all the more lost for their not knowing it.

'Great book, but it's just his vision,' I said.

'It convinces me.'

'It would, because it's close to yours.'

Peter and I looked at each other across unimaginable distances. We live in such proximity and are appalled to discover we could as well be on different planets – more accurately, on the same planet in parallel universes that never quite meet.

Apparently the key to designing a good tea bag is achieving *the right degree of porosity*. Yes indeed. Too much openness, and the world and other people's opinions swamp you. Too little and your world is very dense, dark, and slightly mad.

Andy stretched and got to his feet.

'Time to fish, people! The sun's gone in and there's a whopper waiting just behind that little island.'

As I stand on a new rock and work my line out, I am casting another alongside it, a ghostly internal counterpart, sent out for its own ghostly catch. Which is where we live, balancing precariously on this rock, at the intersection of the world outside and the one within. This rod is real – Korean fibreglass, grey, fragile as it is whippy. It is also an antenna, an aerial, a dowsing rod twitching to the hidden flow.

Which is why I'm smiling inwardly as I retrieve and cast outwardly over the shining lochan. Sebald's vision, his version of European cultural history, of Life itself, is of it as fallen, doomed, disintegrated beyond repair. And why shouldn't he have a vision, a take on the way things are? After all, everybody has to have one, however dim, diffuse or incomplete.

It is not because I prefer my own that, respectfully, appreciatively, I put his vision in its niche somewhere along the whispering gallery that passes for my memory. (It sits opposite the kist containing Norman's vision of salt and honey, of loss and joy inextricably bound together, as conditions for each other.) The reason I do that, rather than submit to or take issue with it, is because it is only a way of seeing, a version.

It seems we have to have one – but we don't have to wholly believe it. That way there is the possibility we may peek round the side of our vision – like Bogart as Philip Marlowe in *The Big Sleep*, looking over the top of his fake reading glasses at the girl in the bookshop while the rain pours down outside. Then we may briefly, flirtatiously, glimpse the way things really are, even as she reaches for the bottle in the drawer and draws down the blind.

Cast: a moment of truth

The lochan, which has been lovely and dead as Lewis on the Sabbath, abruptly comes to life. A squirm of movement, a flicker, then the sound of fish hitting water. We all look up, look to each other as the rings spread. No one speaks, but from our different shores we go to it with a new urgency.

Another rise, this time in the shallows near Andy. He switches his casting inshore. A minute later, a silver-brown surfacing, out by the little island. Somewhere above, AK is rubbing his hands, MacCaig is honing his sarcasm.

'Hah!'

Twenty yards along the bank, Peter has bent forward. So has his rod. It springs sideways, down, across. He reels in, pauses, lets the fish run, struggling to keep his rod high.

I drop mine and run along the bank, camera in hand. My instinct to witness, to record. Across the lochan, Andy is watching but still fishing furiously.

Peter is focused as he reels in line, lets the fish drag away against the tension of rod and reel, then he winds it back again. A fish has to be landed to count as caught, and any moment he could lose it. Among mountaineers, a hill doesn't count as climbed until you get safely back down again. 'The top is exactly halfway,' Mal would always remind me on a summit. 'So keep concentrating.'

'Landing net,' Peter mutters.

I hand it to him, take another picture as the rod rises to near-vertical. Then he leans forward, the landing net scoops down, and we have our fish for Norman.

I have the photo onscreen in my shed. Outside the snow has gone, the tattered snowdrops huddle and quiver. In my picture Peter is standing in the first flush of achievement, so recent he has not had time to pretend to be anything other than elated. The wild brown trout bulges the bottom of his landing net. In T-shirt and shades, above his heavy boots and thick calves, he is wearing old shorts that would not disgrace a disgraced 1950s scoutmaster.

Norman wears very similar ones in an old black and white photo I was given later by Wilma Macaskill. His head is swivelled at the camera, hands in pockets, shirt sleeves rolled up, cigarette firmly between his lips; his friend Pollochan stands in front of the croft from which he takes his byname: elderly, thin, dignified, wearing plain old knickerbockers with heavy wool socks, bonnet, heavy glasses, pipe jammed in his mouth, a straw in his left hand.

The shadows are short and emphatic. It must be near midday, and Norman is scruffy, casual, unguarded in a way I seldom saw in Edinburgh. Here he could get away from being Mr McCaig the schoolteacher, MacCaig the poet. Here he could wear shorts, take a dram whenever the occasion arose (and in Assynt it arose constantly), and nobody gave a damn.

I put the two photos next to each other onscreen, forty

years between them and now alongside. Each is so loud in its moment. If some cosmologists are right, all moments in time lie alongside each other, monumental and particular as the Cuillin Ridge. Apparently we suffer from a purely local perspective as we clamber and scramble our way along our lives.

Perhaps this is not merely the fevered imaginings of hyper-mathematicians struggling with String Theory. Perhaps it applies, playful and true as T.S. Eliot working string-patterns between his long pale hands to catch an invisible cat to amuse a child over afternoon tea. Perhaps he is still at it somewhere. Certainly his poems are.

When I look at those photographs and remember again Peter turning to the camera, exultant, my deepest intuition agrees that it is not nostalgia but necessity that implies those moments exist still, are real and solid as the one in which these words are being read.

And the fish itself, the one MacCaig has nearly fallen out of the non-existent balcony in the sky trying to get a better look at? It is fine, slim, solid, perhaps about 1lb. As Peter cradles it in his right hand, the left supporting its lower body, we exclaim at its beauty. Along its flank are four rows of crimson markings each ringed in silver, and then the underlying shades of weedy green. It is lovely and worthy.

I feel, then and now, a pang that it is dead.

'Well done!' Andy calls.

Let it be said that he is genuinely delighted for Peter and our joint project. That generosity is his nature.

Nevertheless he is still working the shallows on his side of the lochan, even more alert now he knows fish are there to be caught and his brother has caught one.

Peter tenderly lays the trout in his fishing bag.

'That's one to make up for miserable dysentery in Bolivia,' he says. 'The next is for Jack and Jamie.'

I take one more photo as he casts, then hurry back along the bank to my discarded rod. Impossible not to look up at the luminous sky, and wave.

Outside the window of this shed, snow has begun falling again, clogging the laurel's green, muting the Edinburgh traffic. Inside, it is late May in Assynt, by a lochan dark and gold-fringed. Over the last year, that place and this book have come to envelop me completely, as a fever does, or a deep forest, or a demanding late quartet. Wherever you look, all you feel and see and hear is it.

For years now I have extolled the virtue and necessity of living here and only here, now and only now – at which I am not good. But something has shifted in me, and I think now the past, both personal memory and that contained in history and geology, is real and matters. It can nourish or poison us, but either way it must be taken on.

Then *is* Now. Even the future matters, for the future could be as real and solid as this moment, only we haven't been there yet, just as that person walking down the street is real and solid long before you bump into each other on the corner and you apologise and as you straighten up, look into each other's eyes with a flash of recognition.

Another rise, a fluffed strike from Andy, and then the lochan switched off. We kept on at it for an hour, slowly patrolling the shore. Wrist and shoulder aching, I took a break, drank tea.

Sixteen years earlier I'd sat at Base Camp below the Mustagh Tower, holding a chunky walkie-talkie to my ear, and heard through static crackle Mal Duff announce *At the moment we're sitting on top of Mustagh.* I'd felt then as I did now, a tingling, joyous sense of something accomplished spreading through my system as though someone had just injected me with a very good drug. But those true highs were worked for, and they never entirely flush from the system.

I would have liked to have caught the fish myself, but our mission was done. I enjoy fishing but am neither skilful nor dedicated. Climbing was much the same – interesting, challenging, testing, revealing, but not everything. My real job appears to be to write it.

So I made my jottings, then sat and watched my friends follow their passion. The rods rose and fell, flogging a shining dead horse. Clouds gathered on the tops, mist began to roll down into the corrie, the east wind got up. The place had turned its face from us.

'Back to Base?' Peter suggested, pulling on his fleece.

'We can come back early tomorrow morning!' Andy called. 'Bet it's good then.'

We broke down our rods, coiled our casts, gathered our stray gear, stuffed our packs, then set off down. At the last small pool, I took one look back and waved goodbye.

Retrieve: end of the line

Only now, sitting in the wintry Shed with those May days on the screen, the geological map of Assynt on the wall and *We have won the land* balanced on the heater, do I finally get the connection between them. With the little hammers of attention, reflection and narrative, I have been mapping the intrusions of memory, the tectonics of a culture, the fault-lines of a life.

Whether clambering over diorite dyke swarms, passing a hand over my lover's face or the chill strata on Knockan Crag, driving through empty glens, considering the metamorphoses of poetry, the quests are aspects of the one quest: to find the faultlines – or if you prefer something more positive-sounding, the *lines of thrust* – that have brought us to where we are.

As we passed the bealach lochan, Peter glanced and saw the duck had quit its nest on the little island. The gulls must have got its eggs. But he had a trout in his fishing bag and the elements of a new novel in his head. No more would gloomy uncles leadenly ponder their thwarted existence while sweatily rebuilding doomed churches in Bolivia, or smoke their damp, celibate pipes by the turpid Tay. No, this novel would have narrative drive, drama, action! It would be a new kind of novel for him, the publishable kind.

Andy was planning ahead, to meeting up with Andrea, to the meetings he had to set up in New York next week. If he got up extra early tomorrow, he could be up at the Green Corrie just as the morning warmed and those big, fat trout began to feed. Still, *mission accomplished, pal*!

It was becoming clear to me that, if we stayed together, my time for having children had passed. Lesley had her three boys, had turned forty, had done all that. In the first months we talked about the child of our own our bodies clamoured to make. Now we were on the far side of some col, and neither of us knew the ground that lay beyond.

Stay with my beloved and from an evolutionary point of view, I was a dead-end. It seemed a pity. Or, as we three clambered homeward over an outcrop of diorite sill, late intrusion from 2.8 billion years back, completely irrelevant.

When we lay belly to belly in each other's arms, there still came a deep easing, a calm, as though we had ducked out of a turbulent wind. At such moments Deep Time itself was an irrelevance.

Then, below me on the descent path, in a spotlight of sunshine by the burn, Andy turned.

'We did it!' he called, and held his arms out wide.

Peter and I whooped back some pre-syntactic holler of triumph, as though we were galumphing home to our settlement with a haunch of mastodon that would feed the clan for a month, rather than one medium-sized trout.

Exclaiming happily, we continued on down.

Cast: a change of scene

In a made-up story, we would have sat round the camp fire that evening, eating charred trout, toasting with whisky the sunset branding the flank of Quinag, and there you could have left us, happy and resolved.

Fact is, the light turned grey, the air was chilly by the tumbling burn. As we hurried along the shore path by Loch na Gainmhich, our tents looked dreary. When we slung down our packs, we had no whisky, warmth or wine.

The suggestion, I admit, was mine.

We had forgotten about television, flickering the news above the bar. We had forgotten about Guinness, the yellow-white thick heads gathering under the pump. We had forgotten about people, so many, so varied, so loud. We had forgotten about music, and how to disentangle 'Get Back' from the details of the current war.

No doubt, the little Kylesku Hotel was a shock. We sat at a table by the window, raised our glasses to MacCaig, his friends, the Loch of the Green Corrie. We dedicated our second pints to 'the real world', though we remained ambivalent as to whether that was Manhattan or Achiltibuie, London or Lochinver, Sheffield or Suilven.

After the last two nights of dall, chorizo and rice, we had forgotten about pan-fried langoustines, turbot in hollandaise sauce, venison casserole and crème caramel. We succumbed, put in our orders and went outside with our first bottle of white burgundy, and sat watching arctic terns fold their razor wings then plummet into the gulf. It is that I remember as much as anything – the beaded glasses shining on the table and the white birds shafting down like missiles in the distant war.

We sat there, buzzing, hypnotised, astounded till the call came and we went inside to eat and drink among all the humanity, music and wordly news.

I surfaced in my sleeping bag, hearing rain. For a while it was muted, like distant, uncertain applause. Then it crashed down. By my head-torch light I could see the sides of the tent bulge and quiver with impact. Dark patches bloomed where the sagging flysheet pressed onto the inner tent. I should have pegged it tighter. I should have resprayed the seams.

Those things we think of when it's too late. Like my pension payments, or the dying agnostic thinking maybe he should have made that deal with God, just in case. But who pursues equanimity when her life is flourishing, who cuts back when his credit expands?

Behind the thunderous rain there was a deeper sound. An old stream bed, buried unnoticed in the heather nearby, must have filled with run-off from the hills behind. It was as well we'd repitched our tents down on the shingle. As long as the stream doesn't run through any of our tents, we should be allright.

I slept.

★

In dreams my legs were being pulled as I lay on the tiles in the hammam in Essaouira.

In semi-wakefulness, my feet were being lifted and gently swayed about.

I was awake in my sleeping bag in my tent and my feet were being pushed up from under the groundsheet. I grabbed for the head-torch and had a look. At the bottom end of the tent the groundsheet was rising and falling. I leaned across and pushed down gently. It yielded but rose either side of my hand, like a waterbed.

I unzipped the top end of the tent, felt for my boots and crawled out into the rain and darkness. The waters were loud all around. I sent the torch beam across heather, looking for the stream that was doing this.

Another torch, a round-shouldered bulk behind it.

'It's the loch!' Andy called.

Fed by the rain and the run-off from an entire mountain, Loch na Gainmhich had risen up the shingle in the night and was now bubbling under our tents.

We woke Peter. We discussed moving our tents back up onto the promontory. It was back of 5 a.m. but still near-dark, rain was coming down in stair rods, we were wet, our sleeping bags were wet . . .

Breakfast in Ullapool!

Exasperated, hilarious, in the pouring rain we took down our tents, stuffed sleeping bags, karrimats, food, clothes, stove, bottles, rubbish into backpacks and carrier bags. Then slipping and squelching on the shingle, shouting instructions, splashing in the loch, we heaved sodden packs onto our sodden backs, tied on bags and grabbed the rest, then staggered cursing and laughing out of there.

A couple of hours later we were sitting, steaming slightly, in the breakfast café in Ullapool. Andy put down his fork and exclaimed 'We forgot the fish!'

It would be lying where we'd left it the evening before, in a bag in the heather. We'd rushed off to Kylesku to celebrate our success, eaten there, got back late, half-cut, in the wet dark, and never gave a thought to that brown beauty, though it was the point of our expedition. Already it would be unfit to eat. It would lie and rot, wasted.

We looked at each other in silence.

We emerged onto the street, walked down to the harbour front. The clouds were being rolled back like hatch covers, sunlight was pouring over the boats and gulls, the Dearg hills at the far end of Loch Broom were silver-veined with streams.

The street was beginning to steam. The Dorward parents had been phoned and were on their way. Tonight I would be in South Queensferry, then on to Sheffield. Soon Peter would be heading back to London, Andy to New York.

We were well fed, nearly dry, we had done what we came to do, and the world looked fresh and good. Yet the thought of that trout fretted at the back of my mind, a carelessness, a waste. It lies there still, among the richness, the laughter, the many reconfigurations of those Assynt days.

A Late Return

Autumn 2008

1,800 feet up

The flower – it didn't know it –
Was called dwarf cornel
I found this out by enquiring.

Now I remember the name
but have forgotten the flower.
The curse of literacy.

And the greed for knowing. –
I'll have to contour again
from the Loch of the Red Corrie
to the Loch of the Green Corrie
to find what doesn't know its name,
to find what doesn't even know
it's a flower.

Since I believe in correspondences
I shrink in my many weathers
from whoever is contouring immeasurable space
to find what I am like – this forgotten thing
he once gave a name to.

WHERE YOU ONCE BELONGED

'Part the clouds, let me look down.
Oh God, that Earth!'

It is nearly midday in late September as I pull into that remembered lay-by off the Inchnadamph to Kylesku road. On my left, Quinag is still MacCaig's 'tall huddle of anvils'. On the right, Glas Bheinn slouches with shawls of rain cloud wrapped about its massive shoulders.

I get out of the car, eyes snagged by sunlight and stiff breeze knotting the surface of Loch na Gainmhich. In my pocket is a £5 fishing permit from the Assynt Anglers Association. The first Assynt Crofters Buy-Out sparked off a series of community buy-outs across Scotland and in Assynt: Glencanisp, Little Assynt, Inverpolly. Now I have no hesitation in paying to fish these lochs.

From the back of the garage that morning I had dug out landing net, reel, fly box, knife and spare casts, all untouched since the move to Edinburgh and the move before that. They were fousty and a bit rusty, but then so was I. The night before I'd nipped round to Peter's to borrow his rod because it broke down into smaller sections than mine, better for carrying into the hills.

My pack is stuffed with fishing gear, spare clothing, waterproofs, food and drink, notebook, camera. I hoist it onto my shoulders. Hip flask: check. OS map 18, spongy and

tattered, still with Norman MacAskill's pencil marks: check.
Compass: check.

I pull my fishing hat down against the breeze, lock the
car with a quick thought to the Metaphysical Policeman,
and set off into the hills.

Perhaps what brought me back was an outstanding issue
of two fish – the one we caught and forgot to eat, and the
one I did not catch.

Eight years had passed since that expedition with Andy
and Peter. There had been time to take some things to
heart; the rest was forgotten. What remained was less accurate but more truthful. Those few Assynt days had acquired
the heightened clarity and resonance of familiar faces seen
from the rail as the ferry moves off.

Since that Assynt trip I had written two more novels,
and began to feel there was something shabby and
undignified in an adult sitting in a shed making things
up. Then I stumbled over a phrase of John Cheever's:
'Literature is a force of memory we have not understood.'

It sounded like a dinner gong to a hungry man. The
Loch of the Green Corrie wasn't finished with me. Things
had happened there that I had not fully understood. The
brief account I had written up immediately afterwards was
journalism: accurate enough, but with the depth of a single
coat of paint.

And so the next project emerged. On this matter I do
not have the dubious luxury of choice. I went into the garden

writing shed. I sat in the wood-smelling silence, surrounded by old notebooks, photos, maps, then shut my eyes.

I called up that distant lochan, black and flaking gold like an antique mirror, looked into it and waited. Waited as a fisherman waits, hopeful yet accepting of whatever turns up.

Good days and bad days, our loyalty lies in showing up by the water, or in letting fingers stumble along the white pebbles of the keyboard. Some days there is no rise. Nothing comes to the lure, or nothing worth keeping. Some hours you sit there, a mass of aching dough, confronting the pointlessness of this pursuit. *If you can't enjoy fishing all day and catching nothing, you are no fisherman.*

And there had been good days, good hours when words were biting. Sometimes whole silvery streams thrashed into my basket to be later sorted, weighed, salted away. In time I made a couple of trips back to Assynt. I camped by Achmelvich Bay, stayed in the youth hostel there, in a B&B in Lochinver, slept a night in Lord Vestey's former bedroom in Glencanisp Lodge (creepy, that empty place, with its echoes and creaks and imagined footfalls).

I had quiet drinks and riotous evenings in the Culag Bar, walked up the Kirkaig river to the base of Suilven in steady rain, meandered half-cut up the Inver on a moonsmeared night. The people I met and talked with enlarged my understanding of MacCaig, his friends, and the context of Assynt.

But this would be the first time I'd gone back to the Loch of the Green Corrie. I had to come and check I hadn't been mythologising it out of existence. And, who knows, maybe catch something. I first came to the Loch of the Green Corrie because of what it meant to someone else. Now I was back for what it meant to me.

The path dips and rises, awkward with mud and stones. These days I use a ski pole to protect a dodgy knee. Peter had smashed his ankle on a long slide down Ben Alder in winter. Now he was back in action, fit but more cautious, doctoring in Edinburgh, unable to take time off work and family midweek to join me. Andy, jubilant to be living in Edinburgh with Andrea after leaving New York for some years in London, then Home, was also too busy to come out to play. In any case, I wanted to do this on my own.

By now I am skirting Loch na Gainmhich, pausing to glance at the soggy mound where we first camped, and the shingle below where we once sprawled, yarned and drank Glenmorangie into the gloaming. Our Metaphysical Policeman stood right here. Norman MacAskill, the last of MacCaig's old Assynt crew, is gone. That fish we left among the heather must have been food for birds, its fine white bones sunk among the peat.

I pause long enough to take it in, acknowledge, then move on along the shore towards the big burn that tumbles down from the higher lochans. These days it's not so much that I am in a hurry, more that I see no reason to hang back. More than anything, I am finally done with second-guessing my life.

*

Kirkwall airfield is set by the sea in one of the most mist-prone parts of Orkney, and without full radar our incoming flights are regularly cancelled. This gives us the grim pleasure of having our belief in the idiocy of planners confirmed.

Yet the heart too has its most intimate traffic flow through its most occluded parts. That misty morning I walked along the nearby beach, listening to Lesley's plane approach then circle overhead. I could see the control tower, then I couldn't. The plane came louder, the runway briefly cleared then disappeared. The engines grew fainter overhead. Another couple more failed passes and it would head back to Aberdeen or Edinburgh.

It would be her fourth year of coming to Orkney for the October Break, and just a few months after the Assynt fishing trip. Our pattern was still to spend a few vivid weeks together, then go back to our semi-attached lives. As I stared up into the obscurity, cursing it, I wondered how much sense was left in the way we lived.

The engines sounded louder, low out to sea. The breeze tore a hole in the haar, the runway appeared then so did the plane, directly overhead.

Laughing at that moment of clarity, I ran for the car.

Lesley had been ill before, though never as badly as this. She drank a great deal of water and took painkillers. White-faced, she sat up in bed clutching a glass and staring at the wall.

It was a long long night. Sometimes she dozed. Sometimes I slept.

After breakfast I'd left her in bed, dazed with codeine and sleeplessness. It was such a fine morning that on impulse I went out to the Ness to take a short walk by the sea, to take a break and calm down. I came back in the door and heard a sound, like a squeaky toy whose battery is nearly flat. *Heeelp mee . . .*

She was lying by the bathroom door, trying to call through the wall to our neighbour Calum. I knelt and pulled her in to me. Spasms jerked through her legs, her arms. Her pale skin had gone putty-grey. Between quivering lips she muttered the most naked words a human being can say to another.

I'm frightened I'm dying.

It still makes my hand shake to write this.

I got a dressing gown on her, half-carried her down the stairs and out to the car. In my absence she'd collapsed, found she couldn't stop these spasms or get down the stairs to the phone. All the time I'd been strolling along the Stromness shore, admiring the morning.

I walked her from the car through the surgery doors. As the woman at reception looked up, Lesley slithered to the floor and lay twitching. Someone shouted, the doctor appeared, then things happened fast.

She lay on the couch, oxygen mask on, eyes unfocused, face that terrible non-colour. Her hands spasmed on mine then went slack as the doctor rigged up an antibiotic drip, then a saline one. Renal shock, he explained. The jerking was a classic presentation.

He injected a sedative into the back of her hand. 'Her

heart is fine,' he said abruptly. I knew it was, but she had gone so distant and faint. All her force had turned inward, fighting what was happening to her.

I held her flaccid hand. As she had held mine in Intensive Care two years earlier. As I'd held my father's the afternoon before he died. It's all we can do.

'What is your wife's birth date?' the receptionist asked.

'She's not my wife,' I said, then gave it. Lesley's hand twitched, flopped like a pale fish drowning in air.

'Who is her next of kin?'

That simple, bizarre question. I thought of Sorley MacLean's *Who are your people?* But I'm from the East Coast, I don't have people, only immediate family.

'Her mother, I suppose.'

I watched her breathe as we waited for the ambulance. At such times even non-believers call out inwardly to something.

The ambulance came, they transferred her to a stretcher and carried her in. I carried the drips and the oxygen on their little gallows. She looked up at me, gripped my hand and shook so violently they had to hold her on the stretcher. 'We've got to go,' the ambulance man said. I nodded dumbly. 'Fetch her things and follow on.'

I put slippers on her white feet, took a last look, then ran for the car.

That drive from Stromness to Kirkwall took twenty minutes. I tried not to think anything. Just drive, don't have an accident, get there. But inevitably I thought of Norman, going to see his seriously ill wife in hospital.

I will not feel, I will not
feel, until
I have to.

I hurried down corridors, trying to listen when people gave me directions. Finally, a small curtained area. A nurse asked if the patient was family, then shrugged and let me in.

Small tremors still ran down her arm, her eyes were closed but she was no longer grey. Soon as I saw her, I knew she'd be all right. This non-believer looked at her then out the window onto an ordinary day's light falling on an empty car park, and said *Thank you*.

When I left a few hours later, she was awake. The drips were still attached but the oxygen mask had been taken off. She looked at me.

'We can't go on meeting like this,' she whispered, and almost smiled.

She meant, I know, one finding the other in a hospital ward. A sort of a joke. But driving home slowly, exhausted, through the lovely, indifferent light of late afternoon, I knew she was right.

Crossing the Alt Loch Bealach a Bhuirich in spate, then climbing steadily up beside its flashing fall, I recognise that the time when I was much obsessed by death, my own and others', has passed. On our first Assynt fishing trip, not that long after I'd nearly died on a hospital trolley, it was on my mind so much, draining light out of the brightest day.

It made the world insubstantial, so fleeting it was scarcely there, impossible to invest in or get excited about. Which may be wisdom, but my God it gets dull.

I pause by the little waterfall to look back over Loch na Gainmhich, across to Quinag's slumped stone tent. The wind is strong and chill up here, coming from the south-west. Cathel MacLeod, secretary of the Assynt Anglers Association, had been adamant this morning in Lochinver as he'd sold me the permit: 'If there's a wind from anywhere but east through to north-west, casting in the Green Corrie becomes impossible.'

Which was contrary to Norman MacAskill's 'If the wind's from the east, it's no use.' I wonder now if it was an old man's confusion or his mischief. Still, after months of living by the Loch of the Green Corrie in my mind as the book grew, even if fishing turns out impractical, it is time to reconnect to the real thing.

Which, whatever they say, does exist. Even if it evades you whenever you open your mouth.

It was a grand autumnal Orkney day as we drove to Bay of Skaill, her choice. Wide gleaming sky above, its light doubled on the sea, redoubled in the inland waters. And light again in my beloved's eyes. She was chatting away, animated by her first outing since leaving hospital. I was preoccupied, didn't say much. Eventually she was silent too.

We left the car, crossed the little road and came out above the curving bay, the smoothed grey shingle stones so heavy and calming in the hand, wide pale sand, then the water turquoise, a few flickering lines of white, then deeper blue.

Skara Brae crouched among the low dunes at the far end, with its individual cells of red hearths, stone beds, stone dressers with shelves and nooks, sewage and security arrangements (a great pivoting stone slab, a wooden bar fitted across behind). State of the art, de luxe housing community in *c.* 2800 BC. The climate was a few degrees warmer then; it was the land of milk and honey, and with global warming may be so again.

At either end of the flashing bay headlands rose, one with stacks and an arch through which the blue sky glowed. Wide open, yet sheltered and sheltering, Bay of Skaill is the most harmonious, resonant place I know. It is my Loch of the Green Corrie.

We stood on the rise. The tide was out. Glittering blue, white line of tiny surf, green in the lift of the waves. So much clarity.

Some things, once said, cannot be unsaid. It must be memorable. It must be right.

'Listen, I have something to say to you. It's quite important and I need your full attention.' She glanced at me, alert, puzzled. I hesitated. 'I'm sorry, there is no other way of saying this.'

'I'd better move so I can see you better,' she said, and crossed over to my left side so the sun wasn't in her eyes. 'What is it?'

'I've been thinking about this for a while now, it's important you know that. I'm not messing about. I mean this. I can't keep it to myself any longer. Whether you like it or not, it has to be said.'

Now she was looking truly concerned. 'What is it?'

'Well, there really is no simpler way of saying this . . .' A heartbeat pause. 'Will you *please* marry me?'

She stared at me. I tried to smile back.

'Yes,' she said, then put her arms round me and buried her face in my chest. Then she stood back indignantly.

'What a bloody wind-up!' she said. 'You had me wondering there.'

'I know,' I said. 'Just thought I'd make the best of it.'

I take the upward path steadily, carefully, knowing after lots of little injuries how easily the body is damaged. We lose our lightness on this Earth, no doubt.

Our Leo in his teens jumps downstairs, leaps onto the sofa, goes rolling downhill. He can waste hours, days, online or watching DVDs or plucking idly at the banjo, because time is on his side. He has so much of it he can afford to throw it away. His profligacy with time drives me crazy, but holding cheap what we hold most dear is the luxury of being young.

At the top of the rise I pause for breath, look across at the dark, bleak-shored Loch Bealach a Bhuirich where Peter went fishing alone and saw the way things are in a nesting duck being assaulted by two gulls and inevitably losing. Valid joy in this life, that's what I'm still holding out for. A lightness that is not ignorance, for we are too old for innocence.

As the cloud comes down, it's time to leave this path. I set off across humped rock and bog and turf terrain, over the grey diorite dykes, trying to remember the right way. I start following a wee burn that ends – begins – at a tiny dub. Check the map. Mal Duff used to say 'We're either where I think we are, or we're in some other place.'

I check the compass. He is in some other place, and visibility is now down to twenty yards. The mist is wet, and wind chill numbs my hands.

Grey ruffled water, lisping and chattering, appears out of the mist. A little lochan, then a smaller offspring. This should be the unnamed one on the map that Cathel says they just call 'Little Green'. Apparently a 5lb trout was taken from here. Such a sweet name, and I'm hearing the Joni Mitchell song of that title, about the child she gave away for the sake of her career and creativity.

The map says Little Green is fed by a burn from the Green Corrie. Thinking about damp feet, children I don't have, a pretty tune and the irrevocable decisions we make then find a way to live with, I follow that burn up into the blankness, pretty sure I am where I think I am.

We walked along the beach at Bay of Skaill in a state of daze, energy, hilarity. We went up onto the headland, still talking about where we might live. Orkney? Sheffield? Both? Then it got to money, mortgages, schools. She laughed and cut short that talk. That wasn't what this was about.

I took a photo of her that day, it's on the window ledge

in the shed. On the headland above Skara Brae, she wears a blue fleece jacket over pale blue sweater, sun strong on her face. She looks radiant, gleeful. The blue-grey sea below her is broken, boundless; its horizon is exactly at the level of her eyes, and extends them out indefinitely. The rock stack behind her is strongly lit, and every sedimentary layer of sandstone shows. Cracked and notched, it is a tally-stick of Time.

She sits on the cliff top, transitory, alive.

Writing this in the shed with the March light outside making faint the words on the screen, I can see that life-altering hour had its sources way back. The first Assynt trip with Andy and Peter, with its unlooked-for memories, dreams, stories, incidents, reflections, had been one of those periods when one's past assembles to offer itself anew.

I can feel still the reverberation when Peter remarked 'The measure of a person's life is in the number of hostages to fortune he or she is prepared to take on.'

Something shifts, and only then are we ready and able to reconfigure ourselves. Before her brief, dramatic illness, even as the plane that brought Lesley back to Orkney touched down, I knew I wanted to do it all with another adult human being, this one, while we are still around to do it. I had been my own life's spectator long enough. I wanted a new next of kin.

On the way back to the car, she hesitated then said quietly 'I'm not back-pedalling, but do you mind if I think about all this for a while? It's not something that I've been considering.'

'Yes, of course,' I said. 'I'm not going anywhere.'

Months later she was standing next to me as I dried dishes.

'You know what you asked me a while back? I've been thinking about it, and if you still want to, I'd like to say Yes.'

'You'll have to ask me.'

A short pause for a tussle of wills, but I wasn't going to back down on this.

'Will you marry me?' she asked.

'Oh, all right then.'

'Put down that plate, so I can hit you.'

The wind makes a faint tearing, hissing sound through the heather as it peels the mist away like a bandage, and my feet hasten over ground I recognise. How vividly I picture Norman and AK coming eagerly by these pools, over this last mound. When Andy, Peter and I have in turn gone into the silence, perhaps a few others will come this way because of what is written here, and will come over the rise as I do now, see Lochan a Choire Ghuirm for the first time, and think of us arriving here.

Looking down from a place in which I do not believe, I shall be quite chuffed.

Feeling myself escorted by the past on my left and the future on my right, I come out onto the small promontory at the north end of the Loch of the Green Corrie, set my pack down and confront again the disquieting disjunction between the thing itself and as it exists for us.

In front of me is a lot of water in a hollow.

This morning in Lochinver Cathel MacLeod had protested that the corrie *is* green, but my overall impression is still of grey. Steep grey scree slopes, loose rock, coarse turf. Only to the east does the corrie open, and even there is broken bedrock Lewisian gneiss, a long grey arm stretched out to the hills.

It is austere, indifferent, problematic, unyielding, making no concessions at all.

For months this place has been growing in me. Waking in the morning, or sitting in a shed in Edinburgh, I have felt its presence. I would lie awake at night picturing moon and stars reflected on its surface, with no one there to see.

It is not just the dead that accompany us through life; certain places come with us too. The Loch of the Green Corrie had become my Rorschach blob, my oracle, my revelator, its meaning expanding like rings after the fish has gone.

Now here it is in its unadorned reality, just a ragged stretch of water in a bare place.

I look over the lochan, wondering how to resolve this. If the world were indeed just water in a hollow, it would be a poor thing, and we an excrescence crawling upon it. I know some see it so, and the wonder is not more have killed themselves. Then again, if we saw only the inner, transformed thing, we would become detached from this world, float away like an untethered helium balloon high over vale and hill, singing praises in squeaky high voices.

Let's try this: the gap between water in a hollow and the thing we love cannot be closed. The gap between inner and outer world is the condition of being human. We are born in to that tension and we live by it.

When Lesley and I met after a long absence, no doubt sometimes we were privately disappointed. This was just another human being, a bit tired and irritable from the journey, preoccupied. Then we would walk together, and talk would begin to flow, and little sideways glances, until the heart would open and once again one was walking with the beloved.

So I stand for a while at the Loch of the Green Corrie, letting the place in, like the eye adjusting to darkness till it can see again.

It starts with the sound of the wind, and behind it a silence deep enough to hear my own heartbeat. Water, scree, heather and coarse grass. Bounded sky, far hills. Smell of water, turf, stone. The mild chop and mutter of wind and water. The shifting of light. The unstirred body of water below the surface, the hidden life down there. The weight and presence of this corrie.

In part this lochan works as a mirror, as a lover does. But as useful and as shocking is when it, or she or he, refuses to play along with our narcissism. Its otherness is its truest teaching, a reminder that though we give the world meaning by taking it into ourselves, that is not its meaning. MacCaig's poems confront this obduracy over and over.

So is it still special to me, this obscure lochan with a name that is not its real name? Whatever the answer, it does not cease from being water in a hollow, nor my next of kin from being a flesh and blood bright mortal woman who — my first thought, I confess — happens to look good in jeans.

Yes, it is special.

We married in August 2001, on a sunny, windy day, in a bare room in the Town House, above the harbour at Stromness in Orkney. I was not in a daze. I was all there. I was doing this in the full knowledge of the impossibility of a happy ending. I was about to be fifty and never have children of my own.

I had finally grasped that transience is not the enemy of meaning, but its guarantor.

As the registrar stumbled over her words, and I held Lesley's left hand in my right, with her lads and our mothers and a few friends onlooking, and saw the brightness of the day outside, the people passing by, I knew well that grief and sorrow would flow from this moment as surely as clarity and joy, and I stood smiling, embracing the whole damn precious thing.

The bend of a fishing rod, the soar and arc of Quinag. Private events, public events: a matter of scale and balancing.

On our honeymoon in Brazil that September we stayed in a basic cottage accessible only by Land-Rover or boat. No radio, television, newspapers, neighbours. By arrangement we were taken into Parati to buy provisions. There a man urgently waved to us, insisted we come into his clothes shop. Communication was entirely by gesture. He wanted to show us his television, a small black and white flickering soundlessly in the back of the shop. We watched, baffled, as a toy airplane flew into a skyscraper. The screen flickered, then it went back and did it again from a different angle. Or was it a different plane? *New York! New York!* the man said.

We nodded. Some disaster movie? Were we supposed to be excited? Did he think we were American and was trying to make some connection with us, so he could sell us something?

We watched for a while. There didn't seem much narrative, just the same thing happening over and over. It did not look convincing, yet still we were a little uneasy on the boat back. It just seemed odd.

We had another four days before we got back to Rio, turned on the television. We must have been among the last people in the world to know the new millennium had truly arrived.

The earlier sun is smothered in cloud. I shiver and start assembling Peter's rod, fitting together its five delicate spines. I fit the unfamiliar reel, pull the line through the loops and dip into my box of casts. A fishing rod is nothing next to

Quinag, but here I am lifting it again. Of course one's life is tiny, dwarfed by the world and its burning towers, but still it's ours to live.

Life is often good for us. We have work that demands everything; a feisty terrier to replace the boys who have gone out into the world; a garden, a summerhouse, a shed. Also some time to walk, read, make love in the afternoons. We have each other as nearest kin, sworn loyal. What makes complacency impossible is the knowledge none of this is ours to keep.

The wind gusts, first across my right shoulder, then abruptly into my face. I set off along the shore towards where Peter caught our fish, and with the wind at my back, start casting.

Cathel MacLeod was right. Mid-cast the wind shifts, the line swirls sideways, loses its tension and flicks into the heather.

I go over, free the hooks and start again. Get a few casts in, some rhythm arises and the line starts flying out like good sentences, bright lures kissing the rough surface and sinking, then the retrieve that may intrigue or irritate the life down there. I offer it improbable metaphors, simulacra of food.

The wind swirls round the grey-green corrie, and blows in my face again. I can't cast into this. I see Cathel nodding, 'a most frustrating and rewarding place', as I take in the line and plod back to the other bank. He said that last year someone took a 5lb trout from here. I'd settle for anything that swims.

I hunch there, hat pulled down, jacket up to the throat, waiting for the wind to drop or at least settle in its direction.

In the strange Puritanism of leftist politics of the Eighties, I had a friend who disapproved of romantic love on political grounds. She saw it as bourgeois, reactionary, a closing off from the rest of the world. With the death of organised religion, romance had become the opium of the people. (Looking around at the time, I thought perhaps opiates were becoming the opium of the people.) But we are not hiding, huddled from the world, in a cupboard under the stairs. This late love is a portal, a porthole, a window of opportunity, through which one might pass into a wider world.

There was no moral or social need for us to marry, and we were done with pretty fairy tales. Nor was it for financial reasons, for our scarcely existent pensions.

Because it was not necessary, it was done for itself alone. Like poetry, in whose utterance there is little worldly gain, God knows, so we may trust it. We were now done with *wait and see*. Marriage itself isn't really the point, just its best expression.

Is that an insane thing to do, to give over your heart? I wonder as I struggle to make arm, rod, line and cast harmonise. We all know the final outcome here. Where are we going to find the courage to persist?

Consider the alternative. Keep your heart back, don't feel very strongly about anything or anyone. Don't marry. Don't have children. Have no hostages to fortune. You'll get old and die just the same. Only difference is you never lived much in the first place.

Look at it that way and it becomes possible to jump, eyes wide open, off the burning building of your life. Because you chose it, for the time you have left, the falling is flying.

I need to get this line further out, where the big fish lurk, so I step out onto one rock then the next, steady then let fly. Alone in this high place, casting in this awkward, changing wind, I know that day at Bay of Skaill remains the one choice I have not second-guessed.

It is different being here without Andy further along the shore, Peter on the other bank. That first fishing trip already seems a younger, lighter, more innocent time. Public and private, much has changed in the few years between then and now. The Scottish Parliament bedded in, New Labour won more elections, the world warmed up a little more, as it has before, as the glaciers will return here in time. There were new disasters, more doomed, self-harming wars.

Andy and Peter's father died. My mother is in care and no longer capable of reading or following anything, though she does make some jokes, and enjoys being disruptive, awkward and mischievous after a lifetime of good behaviour. *Don't you fackin sweetheart me, darlin!* She seems to have accessed her inner Cockney. The pain and sorrow in that is not hers. I have to remember that.

Hamish Henderson. I smile as I tug in the line. Poet, songwriter, folklorist, socialist, soldier, internationalist, habituee of Sandy Bells, fabulously flirtatious bisexual, the man who translated and took the German surrender of Italy and stuck it in his pocket. Who bet the money for his Somerset Maugham Award on a horse, won and went back to Italy to translate Gramsci's prison letters. I remember him swaying, eyes closed, passionately leading a stolid academic conference in Aberdeen in the mid-Seventies through 'Freedom Come All Ye'. Later that night Iain Crichton Smith, himself with far too much whisky taken, read all of his 'Deer on the High Hills' in a trance.

Well, they're all gone. They really do not make poets like that now. Not with that passion and seriousness, generosity, sweetness and daftness. It has been my pleasure to acknowledge and praise them, who flyted, fought and laughed over the future of Scotland, Mankind and language and lovers, rather than grants, the canon and university posts. Hamish Henderson was a sweet man, brave, eccentric, passionate, idealistic, devoid of malice.

> *Broken faim'lies in lands we've harried*
> *Will curse Scotland the brave nae mair, nae mair*
> *Black and white, ane til th' ither married*
> *Mak' the vile barracks o' their maisters bare . . .*

And Donald Dewar, he went while leading the Scottish Parliament that he and Hamish (in very different ways!) did so much to make happen. He was Old School too, like John Smith. The professionalisation of poets and politician . . .

World rolls on. This lochan is still here, maybe a degree warmer, though none of the water can be the same as last time we were here. A loch is essentially a bath with the tap running and the plug out. We are not so different.

Let me not stand here and *deplore*. We are in danger of doing what we swore we never would when we were young, saying that the world is all changing for the worse.

Dangerous, doomed and horrendous, or beautiful, mysterious and magnificent beyond reason – one's take on the world says more about oneself than the world.

And let me not end up wringing my hands over all who have gone. They in their time were doubtless thought not a patch on their predecessors. The past is a bourach. Let's pay homage, cut off the useful hooks and tie them to a fresh cast.

Edwin Morgan, the last survivor of that remarkable generation of poets, in his mid-eighties wrote a poem entitled 'New is best'. He meant it. An adequate homage to him would be a book all of its own.

Time to try somewhere else.

I've never fished from here before, at the southern end of the corrie. Towering at my back, the scree curtains wrap round two-thirds of the lochan, like the grey-green curtains drawn about my hospital bed, long ago when I was a sick man.

The open aspect is now on my right, where the land

falls away, out into the distance. From here this lochan is not so much hidden in a hollow as reclining on a high balcony.

And the water, which from the other shore impatiently swatted away the light, has become transparent. 'Gin clear,' Cathel MacLeod had enthused this morning. 'It has the finest water quality of any loch in Assynt, with a perfect ph of 6.4.'

I'm smiling as I retrieve, remembering the story Cathel had suddenly come out with. In answer to my question, he'd said he knew AK MacLeod and Norman, as did everyone in Assynt, but not well, for they were of another generation.

'AK was a magnificent caster,' he said. 'Only he could win the casting competition at the Games.' He paused. 'I learned that the hard way.'

Something in his voice alerted me. With a little prompting he told me how once, in the early Seventies, he had out-cast AK at the Lochinver Games. Absolutely no doubt about it, nearly forty-five metres.

MacCaig had been the judge that year, and Cathel stood open-mouthed as Norman took AK's line between thumb and forefinger and walked out to the end of the cast, straightening it, thus lengthening it. He then, quite straight-faced, announced AK the winner.

Young Cathel had gaped, looked around. Everyone could see what had happened. No one said anything. Thirty-five years on, I could hear incredulity, annoyance and amusement still competing in Cathel's voice.

Was that the same legendary year Norman won a gallon of whisky, mounted the cask on the back of AK's old jalopy and they drove round the gathering dispensing joy till everyone was drunk and the cask drained?

Cathel smiled, shrugged. 'That's how they were, the pair of them.'

While remembering Cathel remembering, I am looking right through the water surface to long wavering tendrils of green ropey weed. Among them, something brown and plump wanders lazily, its mouth pouting . . . I blink. It's gone.

So it's true, there are grand fish in here. That one had to be well over three pounds. Maybe Ewen McCaig and Cathel were right when they suggested Norman valued this place simply because it had big, fat brown trout.

Yet even as I urgently cast and retrieve and cast again around the place where I saw that fish, I reject that explanation. It's far too reductionist, one suited to reductionist people. However clear-eyed and sceptical Norman's mind was, his heart was not reductionist. When his noticing eye fell on a landscape, a loch, a friend, a collie, a tattered rose bush, his child-heart would give them their true size and value. *Only love can fairly hold and comprehend it.* MacCaig hated bombast and exaggeration, but he did not want to shrink the world.

In the end his poetry is not so much a matter of words as a function of the noticing eye, the opening heart, the balancing mind. It is that dynamic which makes the words live, just as Erosion, Sedimentation, Uplift remake our world. Of course, no literary theorist could possibly assent to this.

Their loss, I think, and cast again out towards that flicker.

There's two of me now. One is intent, excited, bent on hooking this trout, heart thumping at visions of triumph. *This would knock his socks off.*

The other, with equal intentness, is following a line of thought-feeling. I've been here often enough now, in different weathers, physically and in my thoughts, alone and with friends, to have absorbed this place. Even as this fresh cast snags the ruffled surface, I am sure: Norman MacCaig loved the Loch of the Green Corrie as the essence of Assynt because of its removal from the world that makes it a world, because of the austerity and difficulty that enhance the place's nature, and on account of certain people who once stood by him here.

The wind has moderated, thin sunshine highlights hills in the distance, out beyond the open lip of the corrie. As I work the line out again, vigorously forearming the rod, I'm casting a new narrative arc for the book.

We make our first homage visits to the Loch of the Green Corrie. After much time, effort and conversation, Peter catches our fish for Norman. We go galumphing home. But still something remains undone. In a late postscript, I come back alone, and in my final cast catch a wild brown trout, preferably one of the big ones. Swell the music, pull back from shining fish to severe but gorgeous lochan, the distant hills flamed in sunset. The last cadences of prose wind down and conclude in some image of non-closure, preferably an action, a gesture . . .

We can't help it, shaping the story of our life even as it is happening. I put fresh energy into casting, sensing that this could be it.

The wind shifts and a flying hook embeds in my hat. I force it out, then walk back round to the little northern promontory. This is where we first came in. This is where, one way or another, it will end.

Just as I left Edinburgh a friend said 'Going for a few days' escapism?' And I said 'I guess so,' and let it go. I'm not big on conflict.

Though in my head things can get pretty noisy.

It niggles still, that remark, even as I finally get my line out again, facing the bleak scree slope, with the light breeze behind. Everything is clear and sharp now – the travelling slash of ripples, cool breeze over my hands, my own roughened skin, smell of turf and heather. I've escaped not from life but out into it.

My arm aches, sun has gone, wind is cold. Absolutely nothing is happening. I keep at it, while mentally constructing another possible ending. Say I try and try but catch no fish. Okay, so I must make a shape, a meaning out of that. Or else I could invent, pretend I caught a fish, then run the scene as above . . .

But we do not talk of 'prose licence', and for a reason.

Some compact of trust between writer and reader must exist here. If I do not catch my fish, that has to be the story. It would be about how we can't always get what we want, but in the trying we may get what we need.

My casts are slowing. I'm a clockwork fisherman running down. I call on Norman and AK, Andy and Peter, Ewen and Cathel and Norman MacAskill, all those who have come here and loved this place, and give it a last burst, a veritable spray of casting.

We see only the effects of wind, the things caught up in it, not the thing itself. I watch the far side of the corrie lose colour, then that end of the lochan darken, become riddled with grey. A pale spiral swirls and flattens, coming this way. A rattling sound, then in a drenching blow the hail squall hits.

I kneel, back turned, numb fingers fumbling at the fine loop that secures the cast to the floating line. Finally it comes free. I wind the cast around sodden cardboard, then bend to dismantle Peter's rod. From the corner of my eye, the sky is near black. Half-melted hail sweeps horizontally across the corrie.

Shoes filling, trousers sodden, fingers turning white in the wet half-gale – it is clear we're finished here. That big fish I glimpsed, almost insolent in its nonchalance, is long gone. But another one that brought me here has been hooked, landed and returned. That will have to do.

Chittering with cold, stepping carefully across the growling burn, a hunchback under my sodden backpack, notebook in waterproof bag and whisky flask bumping my hip, I hurry down through the storm.

FUNERALS, GAMES
AND ILLICIT STILLS

Inverkirkaig, like Achmelvich and Clachtoll, Badnaban and Clashnessie and so many other Clearance settlements across Sutherland, is scarcely a village. Not to an East Coast mind. It is a loose scattering of houses among coarse grass and heather, like grey chips thrown from a rough road by the churning 4WD of History.

As in a way it is. Inverkirkaig formed as a crofting township, product of the Clearances, when the people were forced to move out of the glens to the coastal fringe. There they subsisted on what little arable land could be made among the rocks and bogs, augmented with sea fishing and some poaching on the side. They were also each other's only solace and entertainment.

I parked on a grassy slope off the single-track road that ran down the hill above the glittering bay. The last house was a small, upright cottage with a scraggy rowan tree in front. No garden, no fence, no surfaced road up to the door.

I stood in the sunlight, looking at the bay. No other locality has ever appeared so often and in such detail in the work of a major poet.

I had come to fill in a blank that had hung scarcely noticed, like a daytime moon, over our fishing trip. I went up the bank and knocked on the door of that cottage, to call by arrangement on Angus John McEwan, nephew of AK MacLeod.

A.K. MacLeod

I went to the landscape I love best
and the man who was its meaning and added to it
met me in Ullapool.

The beautiful landscape was under snow
and was beautiful in a new way.

Next morning the man who had greeted me
with the pleasure of pleasure
vomited blood
and died.

Crofters and fishermen and womenfolk, unable
to say any more, said,
'It's a grand day, it's a beautiful day.'

And I thought, 'Yes it is.'
And I thought of him lying there,
the dead centre of it all.

Norman MacCaig

Grey-haired and round-shouldered, effusive, excitable, within minutes of me explaining my mission, Angus John was passionately engaged in trying to show me who his uncle was.

'You see that rowan?' He pointed to the tree in front of the house. 'That curious twist in the trunk? I saw AK do that when it was just a sapling. He took the two upper sprigs and pleated them, and that's how it has grown. Just the work of a moment, in passing. He did that kind of thing all the time.'

I will never see that tree, the elegant little twist in it, without thinking of those hands, their quick, witty, transformative interventions in the world – the physical equivalents of MacCaig's short lyrics.

Like many poets, I'm sorry to say, Norman MacCaig was not a practical man. Whereas AK, as Angus John rapidly outlined while dithering around making coffee, was a genius with his hands. Could make, mend, transform anything. He built boats, extended houses, repaired tractors, fixed pumps. He made shepherd's crooks, painted stones, did cartoons, sketches, caricatures, watercolours.

In a place full of fine fishermen, he was the acknowledged master. A wonderful left-handed caster. A terrific marksman. All this from a man who worked, when he worked at all, as a roadman – though often as not Angus John would find him lying on a bank reading a book, shovel abandoned somewhere nearby.

Angus John lowered his voice. 'AK was also the finest poacher in Assynt. It was a matter of necessity, you understand, these people had very little. But he also greatly enjoyed it.' He paused, spoonful of coffee poised above the cafetiere. 'My uncle took pleasure in just about everything, and he gave it back to everyone he met. Norman could be indifferent or impatient with people who he felt were not contributing, or were being mundane. And he needed respect. But AK was open to everyone, and so he tended to get the best from them. I think Norman admired that.'

The coffee finally went in, then the water. I was gasping for coffee and biscuits but reluctant to interrupt.

'Norman said he loved your uncle.'

Angus John looked at me, hand poised above the biscuit tin.

'Did he now?' He looked out the window at the bright bay. 'AK was a very lovable man who lit up everywhere he went.'

I hesitated, not quite sure how to put this.

'I've heard it suggested that their friendship was a bit one-sided, and AK was baffled by the strength of Norman's regard.'

Angus John shook his grey head, puffed out his cheeks.

'A lot of people wanted to be AK's best pal, because he relished the world and helped you relish it too. There may have been some noses out of joint when Norman came up for summer and they went off together. They loved debating and arguing about everything under the sun – he was well read, my uncle, knew everything about Assynt but also took a powerful interest in the world – and fishing together, and whisky. Though in their fifties, they were like wee boys together, always up to something, smiling all the time. They just loved each other's company.'

I nodded. Angus John's open-hearted admiration for his uncle and MacCaig was a welcome counter to the occasional undercurrents of unease, or resentment, or disdain at their passionate friendship I had picked up from some people.

We went into the little sitting room. Angus John rambled off to find photos, old newspaper cuttings, sketches AK had done. I stretched yesterday's stiffness from my legs, still trying to come to terms with the mysterious absence of fish at the Loch of the Green Corrie. I looked around the room where so many gatherings had been, so much talk, whisky, story, laughter, song. For the first time it all seemed solid, non-mythical, real. I needed to understand – no, to feel – what had happened here, so I might know better what our Green Corrie mission had been about.

Angus John puffed back in, his arms full of materials.

'Am I talking too much? People say I talk too much.'

'No,' I said. 'This is just . . . wonderful. Please talk some more.'

The day of AK's funeral was white everywhere, snow down to the water's edge. Sun shining, very bright and cold. Angus John had arrived from university down South. The atmosphere was skewed, shocked, unbearable as they waited for the hearse to come and take the coffin. Aunt Kitty was being busy but she was on automatic. Norman was white, haunted and scarcely spoke. After a while Angus had to get out. When he went outside, this is what he remembers, will always remember: dozens, maybe a hundred people out there, standing silently, motionless, facing the house, like

Easter Island statues waiting for something that was not coming back.

The undertaker didn't have a hearse that day, only a Ford Cortina. The coffin was too long to close the boot, so they had to leave the coffin sticking out the back, tied down with string, and the wreath on top of it. Then when the Cortina began to go up the hill out of the village, the coffin lurched and the wreath started slipping down. Someone had to crouch inside clutching the wreath as the car went up the brae. AK would have hooted with laughter.

While his friend Jenny, a geography teacher in Carlisle, sat quietly listening, or went off to do her own thing, Angus John talked, emotional, animated, breathless, jumping from tale to tale. Though in poor health, he seemed to have some of his uncle's energy and unguarded openness.

AK's wife Kitty was a classic Fifer: practical, realistic, hard-working, organised. A good balance for AK's spontaneity, his disinclination to do anything twice, his love of talking all night then setting off fishing at first light, coming home for a late breakfast then going to bed for a few hours before getting up and on with the day. If AK came home late and saw a light still on in the village, he called in.

'When I think of how those men carried on – lovely men, mind you – the wonder is the women didn't shoot them.'

I made a mental note to get Wilma Mackay's take on this when I saw her later. As Angus John talked, I flipped through old photos of AK. A tall, lean man with reddish hair and a perky moustache, in the uniform of the Lovat Scouts – my father's regiment in the Great War. AK training in Canada in skiing, winter mountaineering. Then fighting in the mountains in Italy through that brutal campaign.

Later his moustache goes grey, but the look in the eye remains. Here he is holding a truly huge salmon, taken from the Kirkaig river. Photos of fishing with friends, on the pier at Lochinver, at the Games with Norman looking thoroughly casual verging on disreputable, who was always rather dapper in Edinburgh. A photo of the Summer Hut AK built, where he and Kitty lived each summer while the cottage was rented to supplement their meagre income. Angus John says it was blown away in the Great Gale, points out the window to where it had been.

I'm trying to take it all in, these photos, sketches, cartoons, drafts of debating speeches, while Angus John talks. He tells me he first came to Assynt as a boy during the War, and how different and wondrous a place it appeared. He diffidently offers to read out 'my incoherent attempt to set it down'. As he reads I look out the window at the bay, at the rowan tree, the shining green vacancy where the Summer Hut had stood, at the empty single-track road where a hundred people once stood like Easter Island statues on a bright, snow-bound morning.

IN PRAISE OF ASSYNT

Earliest memories: evacuation from London at the outbreak of the Second World War and me fast asleep in the slow rocking rhythm of the train north from Inverness. Wakefulness at Lairg. The Post Bus full of chickens, papers, parcels, letters and greeny, purply people some of whom are not speaking English but seem to understand each other. A great, long, meandering journey set to the rising and falling of the straining engine. The driver flings out the chickens, the papers, the parcels and letters to the left and right of the bus, to isolated houses and tiny settlements. Suddenly there is that mountain, Suilven, which holds my eyes for reasons beyond me at the time but that I will later translate as strength, peace, majesty and beauty.

Then it's uncles and aunts and collie dogs and sheep — yes, *in* the house. A grand uncle who looked like Elgar in knickerbocker trousers and his wife who wove thread from wool on her spinning wheel. The sound of waves to rock me to sleep at night and the next day that incredible, varnished, clinker-built wooden dinghy that skimmed through the waves like half a hazelnut shell.

As a nine-year-old I remember the commotion in the house when all the lights went up and there in the moonlight stood my uncle AK holding a 39 1/2lb salmon that reached up to his waist. Grand-uncle Roderick was shaken but not stirred, since his record of 41 1/2lb remained intact.

Memories of days spent out at sea with the men catching fish for the community. This bigger, stouter boat, turned over for the winter would let water pour in until the planks expanded. Over the side you could see the sandy bottom of the bay sink ever further and deeper away. The older men calmly baled away, puffing on pipes or cigarettes while the clear water built up my sense of terror. All was salt and fresh air and the rhythmic creaking of the oars. Then feathers or long hand-held lines fill the bottom of the boat till well over our ankles with ten varieties of fish which will be laid out ashore on a grassy bank for division and distribution to the crofts round about.

It was always hell to have to get up and go away from here, to leave behind what MacCaig referred to as this 'draught of pure being'.

Of course the people here had their warts, prejudices and feuds, but admirable strengths as well. The always open door, the sharing of eggs, milk, chickens, fish, honey; the combined efforts on hay, peat, potatoes, fishing, sheep; the extraordinary gatherings around sheep fanks with picnics, collie dogs, whisky, midges as the dipping went on all day; then the hairy, bleating, animal and human cavalcade of lorries that bounced down the road to the market at Dingwall.

They entertained themselves with their songs, stories and music and there was always a welcome for visitors, a kindness, a willingness to share when it might be ill afforded. They often possessed a wit, a learning, a human gentleness, a resourcefulness, independence of mind, a lively naturalness, qualities that also brought the rich or famous here to seek them out and feel proud if they saw themselves counted as friends. If they visited locals in their wood-panelled sculleries, what they remembered was the presence and spirit of the man or woman, not the basic fittings and the exposed pipes.

Dating from times of oppression, when life for most here was poorer and harder, there was still an independent defiance and proper suspicion of norms of law and order. Polite enough, but still defiant, not easily impressed.

Much has changed, but what remains constant is the landscape which affects and interacts with the character and spirit of those who come to live here. The healing air, which holds scents of pine, heather, bog myrtle, seaweed, the warmth of rocks and sand, the coolness of rivers. A warm summer's night in the Kirkaig gorge with a yellow harvest moon. The sheen of light from the sun that reflects and bounces back from grass and water up into your eyes so that you have to close them, bow your head before the blaze of warmth and colours, almost smiling that there can be such beauty on earth.

Angus John's evocation of Assynt through a child's eyes rang true to me. When we first came here on family holidays in the early Sixties, that was how I saw and felt it. It struck deep into me.

Angus John admitted that that world has changed. The way those people lived, thought, acted, has disappeared. Their particular dignity, endurance, wit, seriousness and levity have gone, along with their material poverty, outside toilets, isolation, and part-resentful, part-resigned, quasi-feudal status.

Assynt is no longer an extremely far-off corner of the Highlands, a world unto itself. Drive by an isolated house at dusk and – if there's anyone in at all, for a significant proportion are second homes or for rent – it is unusual not to see the blue TV screen light through the curtains. Most have their satellite dish and computer terminal linking into the wide world.

Yet tatters of that world remain, like shreds of a gorgeous cloak caught on barbed wire. From Ullapool northwards there remains a certain atmosphere, a way of being and relating. A kindliness, a polite reserve that flowers into generosity, curiosity. It's in the love of talk, anecdote, conviviality. It's in the role of whisky, and a certain spontaneity, verging on anarchy, of being. And the land, the mountains, sea and lochs, the midges, drizzle, the luminous stillness of a summer night at Achmelvich – these remain, and enter into us.

On the rare occasions Angus John talked about himself, I realised that this cheery, self-deprecating, chatty, bumbling man had taught Russian, German, French and English, was widely read and travelled. A man of independent heart and mind, he was an active member of Amnesty International, and quietly pleased to have been arrested during demonstrations at Porton Down and Faslane, the Trident nuclear missile base. With his hospitality, openness, love of conversation, regard for learning and human qualities, and disregard for worldly laws and status, he was a living link back to the Assynt MacCaig knew and gave his heart to.

A job, Angus John confessed, was not something one associated with AK. Like many people in this part of the world, he made up his living with a bit of this, a bit of that, and a little bit of the other which was not talked about. Later he was increasingly a ghillie for people happy to pay for his knowledge and skills. Unfortunately, flushed with success, they tended to buy him too many whiskies afterwards.

Which brought Angus – not so much a stream of consciousness as a waterfall – to a night in the Scottie's Bar corner of the Culag Hotel when an obstreperous trawler crew from Fraserburgh were becoming a problem. Violence was in the air. AK and Norman left their seats and went in among the group. AK said something into the ear of the leader; MacCaig stood alongside him, hands in pockets, very casual.

'I don't know what was said,' Angus John concluded, 'but I'm glad it wasn't said to me. Because those wild men finished their drinks and left like lambs.'

Stories, fragments, images of moments, I build lives and books from them as birds build nests from straw, mud and gobbets.

Angus John chuckled. Once when they were walking together along the Kirkaig river, AK reached up into a tree, plucked out a fishing rod, murmured about having some business to attend to, and disappeared round the bend. He came back five minutes later with a salmon and a big smile. Hid the rod in the tree, the fish in the recesses of his jacket, and they went home. 'He was like that, a magician.'

I mostly forget what happened yesterday or this morning, but I will not forget that incident which I never even saw.

At one of these gatherings Norman was challenged by a very drunk David Rollo, 'Why d'you keep writing bloody poems about fish, worms and dogs? What about politics, the world situation, important things, not damn ducks!' He grew so excited in his chair that he fell out of it backwards, out the open door. They found him lying passed out with his head in the bathroom, his feet in the hall. 'Well, I don't think we need pursue that one any further,' MacCaig drawled, and they went back to carry on the evening.

MacCaig could be very cutting. He could go too far. Angus John leaned back in his chair and told me of the night in the Summer Hut when Norman, too much drink taken, had had a go at an evangelical Christian college friend of Angus John's. Told the man he was an idiot, a naïve fool, and not to bring his poisonous beliefs in here.

It had gone beyond flyting, this was personal. Angus John saw his aunt's lips purse; she caught AK's eye. Norman was taken outside where AK told him the man might be a fool but he was a guest in this house and was not to be spoken to like that. MacCaig stood there. He was not normally spoken to like that either. Then he went back inside, head bowed and said – mock-humble, drolly penitent, but he said it – 'I'm *sorry*.'

'These are just wee stories,' Angus John said apologetically. 'If you want dates and places, accurate details like that, best ask Wilma Mackay.'

'Stories are just fine,' I said, still boggling over the notion of anyone telling off MacCaig. How he must have respected AK and Kitty to have taken it.

'Kitty was older than him, possibly near forty when they married,' Angus John said as we ambled out of the house. 'Those women were absolute power stations of sustenance and stimulation to all the excitement going on around them. Indispensable.' He paused, one hand on the window frame his uncle had made. 'They had no children, but Kitty had two miscarriages. I knew that somehow, but it was not talked about. People kept their sorrows to themselves then. Maybe too much so.'

I nodded, thinking this was not negligible information. It added a dark outline around such brightness, defining it.

We stood where the Summer Hut had been. Angus waved his arms, emotional, animated, zipping off at tangents. So many wonderful evenings in that tiny, Spartan place! Aunt Kitty drinking her thimbleful of whisky to be sociable and bringing in the sandwiches.

What did they do? They talked, they blethered, told stories and jokes new or familiar. Also on the menu were gossip, rumour and passionate disputation on everything from pacifism and the nuclear deterrent, to the best way to deal with ticks and absentee landowners. If pushed, MacCaig would recite 'The Lums of Balgeddie', never his own poems. He sang *Oh the moon shines bright on Charlie Chaplin/ His boots are cracking for want of blacking* . . . Some fine women singers sang Gaelic airs and brought a brief hush.

'Though it was tiny,' Angus John concluded, staring at the spot where the hut had been, 'every summer the hut became this wonderful meeting place where people talked and laughed, sang and drank and talked some more. These people were anything but the taciturn Scot everyone imagines, so canny and careful and unexpressive. They were being Gaels, a different thing altogether.'

When Angus John was old enough, Norman took him for a day up the Kirkaig river and taught him how to fish properly. It was hot and the famous poet wore a knotted hankie on his head. He was a beautiful caster, effortless and precise, almost as good as AK.

'People kept offering AK better jobs, but he always managed to slip out of it. Wise man, I sometimes think. Once, poaching on the hill, he shot off a stag's jaw. He pursued and pursued the wounded animal but couldn't track it down. He never shot deer again.'

He paused, head bowed, remembering. Then he laughed. 'Norman loved to tell how after an unproductive afternoon's fishing, AK cut a small piece off one of his wife's plastic macs, bound it to a hook, cast – and in five minutes he'd got his fish. And a row from Kitty when he got home. Improvised, you see. His whole life. He loved Paul Robeson.

Dogs worshipped him. He lived for the present moment,
nothing more. Quite rightly! More coffee? A dram?
Biscuits?'

All seemed a good idea, but for now it was better to
stand with Angus John, near the tree AK had pleated, on
the spot where the Summer Hut had been, and quote the
ending of Norman's poem about it.

> If I were a bethlehemish star I'd stand fixed
> Over that roof, knowing there'd be born there
> No wars, no tortures, no savage crucifixions.
> But a rare, an extraordinary thing –
> An exhilaration of peace, a sounding
> Grace with trinities galore – if only
> Those three collared doves in the rowan tree.

The other person of AK's stature in Assynt, Angus John
offered, and I realised I'd heard this before, from
Norman – during another evening by the fire at Leamington
Terrace – was Charlie Ross. A large, heavy man, he radi-
ated presence, warmth, good humour and conviviality. Like
AK, he sang beautifully. He and his first wife held legendary
informal gatherings, suppers that became wonderful ceilidhs
that could go on till dawn. He too was memorialised and
celebrated by MacCaig.

Charlie Ross was head keeper at Inveruplan, which didn't
get in the way of his comradeship with AK. They tacitly
agreed to keep off each other's territory. Once AK was
caught deer poaching by an overly keen young keeper –

Charlie Ross apologised later to AK that he had been unable to prevent it.

Excited, distracted, Angus John looked out the window on the glittering bay at things and faces no longer there.

'It's a pleasure to talk of those people again,' he said. 'I think they were special – but then again, perhaps everybody thinks the people and places they live in are special.'

'If only they did,' I replied.

'Charlie Ross and AK were exceptional men in a place full of big characters,' he said. 'Norman thought so too. He believed Lord Vestey was nothing compared to them, a nobody. I agree! When Kitty died later, their whole estate amounted to £280. That has always seemed strange to me, when in terms of life given, love, esteem and affection generated, my uncle and aunt were so wealthy.'

A moment's silence while Angus John poured coffee and muttered through his cuttings and Jenny put some more coal on the fire. Now I could make more sense of AK's attraction for Norman.

In the world of words, our only competence, writers often feel themselves insubstantial and phoney, operating at one remove. MacCaig's poems wrestle with this over and over: the word is an arrow that will always miss its mark. 'The curse of literacy'.

Novelists may bemoan the impossibility of grasping or relaying character, or the lie of narration. Poets distrust, are impatient with, at times resent, their own capacities of word and sound and image. In the arts their highest regard commonly goes to music, as did MacCaig's. And we admire physical competence, and those people who radiate a sense of being utterly at home in the material world.

Perhaps we envy them too. I have never met a joiner who distrusts his own capacity to make things fit, or a plasterer who looks at a finished wall and thinks *That isn't what I meant at all.*

Norman MacCaig was self-conscious, aware of his awareness, always at one remove, observing. So he was drawn to men like AK and Charlie Ross, women like Kitty and Flora, who seemed to have the gift of self-surrender and unmediated being, the capacity to connect directly with people and the world. Of course he loved them, as I have loved physical, emotional men like Graeme and Mal Duff. Or Don Coppock, who fought the fight that had to be fought, but didn't let it consume his life.

In our hearts we know what we are lacking, and are drawn to those who have what we do not, as though through proximity their particular sweetness of being may rub off on us.

Diffidently, I raised the drinking. Someone had muttered scornfully the other day 'AK and MacCaig and these people who were supposedly such "characters" were just half-cut most of their waking lives.' The man who said this looked like a drinker too, and I suspected from his voice he'd once suffered the crueller edge of MacCaig's tongue.

Angus John seemed unoffended. Certainly AK had a boundless appetite for whisky and company. He drank for social conviviality – probably too much in his latter years. Angus couldn't imagine him drinking alone. Then he laughed and admitted AK didn't need to, because he wasn't all that often alone! Whisky, he emphasised, was totally part of the fabric, the context of life here. It was almost . . . sacramental.

Some people were known to have gone too far. They were the ones who drank secretly before turning up, or went on drinking after everyone had left. That was regarded with sorrow and regret, a waste – for what possible pleasure could there be in drinking alone?

AK and Norman and Charlie Ross once decided to distil their own whisky, did I know that? Davy Kirk the Coatbridge plumber, who seemed to be in some compe-tition with MacCaig for AK's company, made the condensing coil. They called it Corbie Whisky, after the pet crow Charlie Ross had. 'What kind of gamekeeper keeps a pet crow?' Angus John exclaimed.

He came up for the Games one year and Charlie Ross beckoned him over, taking him round the back of his Land-Rover to slyly produce a whisky bottle filled with clear liquid. 'We kept this one for you.' *White whisky* it is called in the Highlands. Angus insisted it was wonderful stuff; next day Wilma Mackay would laugh and said it was foul, undrink-able.

He remembered MacCaig in Assynt as boyishly happy and relaxed. 'Norman rejoiced up here. With his Rolls-Royce brain, he couldn't quite be the fisherman's mate, but he tried his damnedest. Never patronising, often admiring. He flowered in their company.'

In Assynt MacCaig didn't have to be the schoolteacher, the poet, the public person. The suit, the pose, the urbanity were discarded for shorts, scruffy sweaters and mud-caked shoes. Only the whisky, the fags and the noticing eye remained constant.

Mostly Jenny sat quietly, occasionally correcting or prompting Angus John. She had been coming up here for some twenty years, had not known AK but had met Norman a number of times. 'Some people found him a bit intimidating, but to me he was perfectly friendly.'

She couldn't remember the first time they'd met, but she remembered the last, and it has stayed with me.

He was old then, on one of his very last visits to Assynt. They'd had an evening's meal and conversation, and when she and Angus were ready to leave round 2 a.m., Norman insisted on walking them down the path to the gate. There was a gale, and a very bright moon, and his long white hair blew wildly up over his high-domed forehead. 'He looked extraordinary,' Jenny said. She said he called out 'Ta-ta, ta-ta' as his last goodbye.

When she'd looked back at the end of the path, he was still standing there looking at the night, his hair blowing up in the moonlight, his deep-set eyes pools of darkness. 'I'll always think of him like that,' she said. 'Like Moses looking out at the Promised Land.'

We have talked way past lunchtime. I need to leave, eat, recover, sit somewhere quiet and enlarge on my few scribbled notes. Angus John comes outside with me. We shake hands warmly. He will look for more material on his uncle, says how much he's enjoyed talking about him and those people and days.

Before getting in the car, I take a last look around at the bay, the sunlit cottage, that rowan tree, the few scattered houses. There is the green patch where the Summer Hut stood, blown away in the Great Gale. A much quieter gale has carried off its inhabitants, one by one.

There has been sorrow in these Assynt conversations. But I have also seen in others' eyes the pleasure of recalling and memorialising cherished people and times. Only once the last people who remember it have gone will the Summer Hut have been truly carried away, along with those who once passed the time of their lives there, within the flimsy walls that AK built.

It was late afternoon when I got to Wilma Mackay's house after the eventful three miles of looping, blind, improvisational single-track road back from Lochinver. Hard to concentrate on the road when mountains and lochans and glowing slopes and glittering river kept appearing, briefly framed, then vanishing again. First streaks of snow on Suilven and Canisp, more on Quinag. The sky that hard wintry blue, the sun getting low and buttery.

I was low-blood-sugary, head still stuffed with Angus John stories and images and emotions. I had gone back to town to eat something, found no hot food available, had a quick sausage roll from the Spar shop. All the tourists had gone, the B&B signs taken down, even the Caberfeidh pub was closed. My time here was almost done.

Wilma opened the door, grey-haired, quietly smiling, at once formal and warm as she asked me in. On this my second visit she insisted on making me ham rolls and pots of tea – 'I would offer you a dram but you're driving.'

While she was in the kitchen I looked along the shelves crowded with photos of children, weddings, grandchildren; older pictures of her with a sturdy man with thick dark Andy Stewart hair brushed back from his forehead: George Mackay her husband, owner and manager of Lochinver Fishing, friend and whisky-companion of AK, Charlie Ross, MacCaig.

On my last visit I had talked with her about my conflicting feelings on the central role of whisky in these parts – tragic symptom and sole consolation of the culturally, economically, politically and linguistically dispossessed, or indeed the water of life, the sacrament of good company and human gladness?

The issue had been increasingly on my mind. I have long enjoyed beer, wine and whisky (let alone gin, brandy, cider and dry martinis). I like the taste and I like the early effects, the warmth, expansiveness, well-being. But I'd be a useless drunk because after a certain hour and a certain number of drinks, I have had enough, whatever the company, the wit, congeniality and apparent brilliance of the evening. Norman loved to tell the story of being with Sorley MacLean at some gathering. 'Norman, if I had Helen of Troy on my left and Voltaire on my right – still I would rather go to bed.' I'm with him on that.

AK died earlier than he should have through whisky, as did his father, and Sidney Goodsir Smith, and several other friends of Norman. MacCaig somehow it had pickled and preserved. His son Ewen pointed out that he never saw his father drink alone, and normal family meals never had alcohol with them, so he had long breaks for his system to recover.

It goes right back to James Hutton as a student in pre-Enlightenment Edinburgh, and how he and his friends regarded the oncoming Jacobites. That internal divide still runs through my country and myself. As an East Coast person who values clarity, rationality and making the most of the time we have, I view reliance on alcohol as a tragic waste. And then I'd come to Assynt, to meet and listen and partake, and become absorbed into that culture, and then my previous outlook seemed prissy and mean-spirited, missing the point, almost colonialist.

Wilma had quietly replied 'There are indeed two ways of looking at it.'

The room was warm, loved and looked after, crowded with mementoes of people and places, friends and family. A great window taking in the light over the bay. A piano, rugs, carpets, books. It was lovely and full of absences. So many meals and parties and ceilidhs had been celebrated here; so much whisky, wine and talk, music and laughter, children, dogs. Happy ghosts, perhaps, but ghosts neverthe-less. Maybe it was just me but it felt like the set of a play that had finished its long, illustrious run.

I hoped it was just me.

We sat on opposite sides of the coal fire in the large sitting room, eating rolls and drinking tea then coffee. She was another very competent East Coast woman, who had come from Aberdeen as a student to work in the Culag Hotel and stayed on. She filled me in on her children, now all married, all left home but one son no further than Lochinver. I felt emotional but somehow secure sitting there, not wanting to leave and drive to my tent pitched above Achmelvich Bay. Like Angus John, though more calm, she was an easy, generous, comfortable presence to be around. In them both I glimpsed something of the world and qualities MacCaig had so loved.

'Angus John says it's a wonder their women didn't shoot them,' I said. From the dubious vantage point of my East Coast moral high horse, those men seemed to have had charmed and essentially adolescent lives. Surely, I said to Wilma, it was all made possible by the women. Someone must have kept an eye on the money, the children, provided the food, cooked, cleaned, helped them to bed.

She laughed. 'That's all true,' she said, 'but women like Kitty and Isabel and Flora, though quiet, were strong people. They had their own lives on their own terms, they joined in what they wanted to join in. They were essential, and they and their men knew it.'

And there were women at these social evenings of whisky and talk? She laughed again. 'How could there not be? The fishing, that was another matter.'

Isabel McCaig used to babysit Wilma's children. She was an Edinburgh Scot, quiet, very bright – 'probably more intelligent even than Norman' in Wilma's opinion – and could be steely in her disapproval, not easily swayed. While Norman was out on the hills, Isabel worked on her etymological research. She had been a significant and highly regarded scholar.

'For me they were a couple, and I thought of them as great friends. You know what I mean.'

She agreed Norman could be cutting, and some people found him intimidating – something in his bearing, his irritation at stupidity or banality. 'I was never scared of him,' she said, 'though he once said I was an elitist snob.'

Pretty strong stuff, I thought, but she laughed quietly. 'I didn't mind,' she said. 'I sensed he was talking about part of himself he didn't like.'

Such clarity and charity. If she said those women were not victims, I rather believed her.

'When I was here the other day,' I said, 'I talked about my ambivalence to whisky culture and asked what you thought. I didn't know then about your husband . . . It must have been upsetting – I'm really sorry.'

She made a small gesture with her hands, so subtle and eloquent I cannot relay it.

'Thank you,' she said. 'What's done is done.'

'Norman was a very good dancer,' Wilma said. 'We had many meals and parties in this room. He would recite ditties and light poems, but never his own. Once when I said he was sometimes a bit rough with people, he replied "Me? I'm gentle as Johnson's Baby Powder!"'

She showed me photos: Norman and AK with friends by the Kirkaig, fishing rods propped on the bank, meals and meetings. The lost world of black and white, men in old tweed jackets, scoutmaster shorts or knickerbockers, pipes clenched in hand or jaw, tweed cap or deerstalker; then the world of altered colours, exaggerated orange and green, knitted wool ties, open-necked shirts, and every hand spiked with a cigarette.

I focused on one of Norman with AK at the summer Games. Norman has a judge's badge on his lapel, is leering at AK who looks glowingly pleased. This might well have been the day that Norman fiddled the judging to ensure his friend's win over Cathel MacLeod in the casting competition.

'They look as if they've been up to something,' I commented.

'They usually did,' Wilma said. 'Usually they had! I know Angus John thinks the world of his uncle, but he really was a wonderful man. I'm glad I had his company the day before he died.'

She had my complete attention.

She had driven to Ullapool to pick up Norman that day in January '76. He was coming up by bus from Edinburgh to attend an Assynt Anglers Association dinner. AK had not been in good health for a while but was keen to see Norman as soon as possible, so he had come along. It had been snowing, and snowed again on the long drive back, with the two men talking animatedly all the time.

Norman stayed that night with AK and Kitty. AK went to bed quite early, saying he didn't feel very well. During the night he had a pulmonary aneurysm – his artery split wide open. He died bloodily, quickly, with Kitty and Norman there.

I knew the poem of that last day and night well, but had never heard the reality of it from someone so close. I'd not considered that MacCaig was in the same house, had been there at his death. Anyone would be shocked; Norman was highly emotional and sensitive under his Edinburgh carapace, and truly adored AK – of course he was shattered. Haunted. Devastated. Nineteen years later, talking of his friend, the pain had been there still, vivid under the arch of his eyesockets, along with the pleasure and tenderness in his voice. Now I was sitting at the fireside of the woman who had been the driver in 'Notes on a winter's journey', the first of the AK elegies.

'He sent Kitty the hand-written group of poems for AK,' Wilma said. 'She was upset by them. She found them in places too graphic. I know Norman meant them as a tribute, but at the time it didn't help. But she would have been polite, and I don't know if he ever knew that.'

I felt some kind of free-hand circle had been closed.

As I drove back to Lochinver through the last light gathered in the tiny roadside lochans, lines of Rilke surfaced.

Work of sight is achieved,
now for some heart-work
on all those images, prisoned within you . . .

I had received so much, had so much to unpack. I was
full of faces and stories from these late visits: Wilma and
Angus John, Cathel, Mandy Haggith and Bill Ritchie who
had talked about the buy-out and given me introductions,
put me up at their 'deconstructed dwelling' on his croft.
Also Wilma Macaskill, Pollochan's daughter, so lively and
funny, telling stories of the joys and escapades of her childhood, of the way Norman's unvarying stride ate up ground
on the hills, how he was a brilliant whistler, how her father
had had eighteen cattle and she only found out later he'd
sold them one by one to raise the money to send her to
a girls school . . .

My head and heart bulged with Assynt like an over-
stuffed suitcase. I was needing food in Lochinver if anywhere
was still open, then a pint, then on to Achmelvich and my
tent. Tomorrow would be time to go home to Lesley, then
unpack it all in the shed.

This shed. Through the window, our improbably angled
eucalyptus tree shudders in the April winds. On my screen
glows one of the photos Wilma let me copy. It was taken
on Norman's last Christmas, at his daughter Joan's house.

I look at it to be reminded of what in the end I take
from Norman MacCaig. When I was a teenager reading
his poems in the *Weekend Scotsman,* I loved his celebration
of the natural world and his delight at being in it. As he

aged and his losses started to pile up, mine were just beginning, and then I saw the dark outline round nearly everything he wrote. His celebrations had become elegies, the dark border got thicker towards the end and the light more hedged in, circumscribed, and that has reflected my own outlook as the years and losses grow.

And now this photo shows me what I am in danger of forgetting. Witnessing and remembering Norman's sorrows and advancing physical decrepitude, and the sadness that brought me − seeing in him so much of my father's late decline, and then my mother's − and then the gaping loss I felt after his death, which brought me to Assynt to honour him, I am in danger of missing his last teaching.

Here he is, this ravaged, aged man, near the end. AK is long dead, as are Kitty and Flora, Charlie Ross, Pollochan, Chris Grieve, Sidney Goodsir Smith, his sister and now his wife. His heart is not good, he cannot walk any distance, he is kept going mainly by pills. It is many years since he has been able to go far from the car and the road, into the hills he loved, to the high lochs he once fished. All that is left is memory, and it brings as much pain as pleasure. There really is little light left.

Towards the end of his last Christmas meal, he is sitting at a table crowded with empty wine bottles and glasses and coffee cups. In front of him, a large tumbler of whisky.

He is looking with glowing pleasure and admiration at his grand-daughter Catherine, a lively, dark-haired woman, the one who most inherited his love for Assynt. She is beaming delightedly back at him. *I am bombarded with things that are lovable.* In a green pullover, one wing of his shirt collar poking out over it, Norman MacCaig is unshaven and raggedy and truly old, yet free and glorious at the table at the end of the feast.

Between mountain and sea

Honey and salt – land smell and sea smell,
as in the long ago, as in forever.

The days pick me up and carry me off,
half-child, half-prisoner,

on their journey that I'll share
for a while.

They wound and they bless me
with strange gifts:

the salt of absence,
the honey of memory.

Norman MacCaig

Trout and invisible treasures

Next morning I crawled from my tent above Achmelvich, brewed up and drank tea while watching an offshore breeze back-comb the incoming waves. It was a bright grey morning that could go either way. I had planned to go home to Edinburgh, to Lesley and our empty nest dog, and a book that needed finished. Instead on impulse I drove back to Lochinver and called on Cathel MacLeod to ask where I might best fish on a day like this.

He came to the door. Caution was replaced by enthusiasm as I talked more about my MacCaig quest. Former policeman, secretary of the Assynt Anglers Association, a neat, lively man with weathered face, he was not surprised to hear we had struggled in the past with the Loch of the Green Corrie, and that I'd had to bail out the other day.

'It is one of the best fishing lochs in all Assynt, and probably the most frustrating.'

He looked out the window at the wind direction, and said the Green Corrie and the Red Corrie would both be hopeless today. On impulse I asked if he had any idea which loch MacCaig had been referring to in his poem 'Rich day'. I quoted the opening.

All day we fished the loch
clasped in the throat of Canisp, that scrawny mountain,
and caught trout and invisible treasures.

Cathel grinned. 'I know that loch.' He opened my old map, hummed as his finger moved. 'There,' he said. 'A good place on its day.' He circled it in pen. Loch na Faoleige.

Mid-morning found me crossing the Loanagh burn in wellies, then looking at the long rise ahead. Slabs of bedrock poked through among broken boulders, glacier moraine mounds, stunted heather, tussocks and turf. After the rain the burn was big; a waterfall flashed through a little gorge near the top. Somewhere over that rise was Canisp and its attendant loch. MacCaig had taken out and renewed his poetic licence many times, but that poem seemed so direct and unadorned I believed it was about a specific place, a specific day. And specific friends in that 'we'. AK? Very likely. A man I could now see more clearly.

I pulled off the wellies, left them in bracken, laced up my boots, and set off on the climb from myth to reality.

I felt well and somehow lighter. Also reasonably fit by now, senses alert, mind running freely as the gurgling burn where I knelt to drink. As I paused by the waterfall the sun came out briefly, a thin autumnal yellow, and a pocket-sized rainbow opened its fan inside the spray.

Good omens everywhere. There were also the fishing lessons I'd had lately from Ian the ghillie at Torlundy Farm in the Great Glen. He had strapped the butt of the rod to my forearm to stop me using wrist action when casting. 'Jist yir foreairm,' he'd instructed. 'Foreairm an shooder.'

And he'd identified why I often failed to secure a fish when one took the lure: tip of the rod too high, too much loose line, so the strike would be limited and late. Some people point you in the right direction, others show you how to act when you get there.

Inside an hour I was clambering over the bealach. Canisp rose hooked and horned on the left, all scree and coarse grass, burn-torn: *scrawny*. A long undulation of peat-hags, hidden burns, mounds and tussocks lay ahead. Take a little care on this ground; this is not a good place to turn an ankle. The responsibility remains yours. Marriage doesn't change that.

According to Cathel, I wouldn't see the loch till I arrived at it. Here was no path, no person, no cairn or dwelling, not even a rickle of stones from a summer shieling. Trusting the word and the map, I went on into the unknown.

And there it was, sprung abruptly from the lines of a poem. Long and slim, casually flanked by Canisp – *clasped in the throat* was pushing it, however elegantly – the loch was blue and dark, brown and clear, chuckling idly to itself as I drew near.

Loch na Faoleige, 'Gull loch'. I loved it on sight.

Through many hours as the sun came and went and wind blew across water and moorland, there was no companion, no human voice. But two hinds raised sleek heads by the loch shore as I approached, jumped up and scuttled away.

In the gravel their elegant prints shone even as they filled in. A flight of mallards went by in Fifties suburban hallway formation. A buzzard croaked in circles until another responded across the hill; they drifted towards each other then were gone. A little fish jumped, a silvery apostrophe marking its possession of the moment.

There was sun on neck and cold hands; wheezing of wind over land; russet-tipped grasses rose through heather and bent in the breeze. Numb fingers cut the line, tied on fresh lures. Water glittered, went dark, shifted to blue, platinum, lead, was clear and brown in the shallows. It clucked, clicked, bobbled on the small stones. Thoughts came and went, clouds opened up, slid back, re-formed. The scrawny mountain held its ground. There was chocolate thick and sweet against the upper palate; stabs of pain under the right shoulder as the casts slowed. There was hope, expectation, boredom, peace. Everything was 360 degrees, all around.

The very grammar changes as 'I' disappears, dissolving into the world like dregs of tea flicked into a loch.

Once or twice in those hours by the lochan below Canisp, I'd remember and look around quickly behind me, startled to realise myself. Here. Alone. Mountain, loch, moor, sky, and little me standing on a rock, sending out a line. Shocking to be so exposed, as if moor or loch might gulp, convulse briefly and swallow me.

The wind bends the grasses, spreads dark fans across the loch, and I am gone again.

*

Back in the world of desire and intention, I was feeling hopeful. Often, in my inexperience and inadequacy, I have cast without much expectation of catching anything. Usually I prove correct in this. Maybe fish sense my lack of conviction, or are put off by my clumsiness. Either way, they do not often rise for me, nibble rarely, are hooked and landed even more rarely.

Why have I continued fishing at all? Because of Mal, because of Norman. Because I enjoy being in a boat drifting across a loch, casting and watching light on water for hours. Even bank fishing offers a reason or a pretext – let's say 'an occasion', in the way that Norman MacCaig may be more the occasion than the true subject of this book – for the walk into the hills, ideally across a pathless moor; there is still the arrival at the loch side, and then the hours of attention and forgetting.

As I worked steadily along the shore of Loch na Faoleige, I felt many circumstances coming together on my side. On these visits to Assynt, I'd put in the time and effort. I'd surely earned a fish through sweat, wet, occasional sunburn, thirst, cold, muscle burn. Earned it by hours' driving and walking, by whisky, conversation, listening, looking, reflecting. By *taking instruction*.

This would be where I'd catch my fish for Norman MacCaig. After all, I'd read and carried that 'Rich day' poem in me for thirty-five years before I'd even heard of the Green Corrie. A fish caught here would round off the quest.

So I cast with atypical belief and attention all the way down that shore, cool wind and warm sun on my neck and hands. Another small fish rose clear of the water at the far side. The flicker of its surfacing, the soft clap of its fall, then the widening ring confirmed this world is everything to me. It always has been, of course, but now the vow has been renewed, consciously made, adult.

The ring enlarged, wider and fainter, till I could follow it no more.

Only now, in late spring, intently watching myself alone and self-forgetting in the hills that autumnal day, towards the end of these late returns, do I see what we've been up to here. Which is tracing ways that we take the world and remodel it within. Call it metaphor or memory, opinion or mind-spin, it remains the incorrigible subjectivity we call our life.

And then there is the world out there, all that is not-ours and not-us, where we are peripheral. Science, with its aim of objectivity and its method of close observation, reasoning and constant testing, gives us some handle on what exists and how it works. With its micro and its macro, its Deep Space and Deep Time, it threatens but cannot entirely overwhelm the personal model world within.

Between the two, the inner and outer worlds, lies a chasm. And across that chasm are slung the slender, dizzying bridges of empathy, metaphor, curiosity, art, intellect and the potency that bundles together all these – love.

Norman MacCaig, and the small undertaking he once asked of me, has brought me to a place not so different from his, but my own.

★

Tiring, I stopped for another break. Ate the dates, the flapjack. Drank the musty flask tea and looked around, behind
me at Canisp rising across the loch. The two buzzards drifted
closer together across the sky and headed north. Abruptly,
intensely, I thought of Lesley for the first time in hours.
Perhaps she had just looked up from her work and thought
of me. I said her name quietly aloud because I'm a sentimental soul and have long ceased being ashamed of it, then
flicked away the last drops of tepid tea and poured some
fresh hot.

There once were summer shielings up here, where people
worked, lazed, courted and minded their sheep and cattle
through the bright months. There's no going back, not
even for Gaels, to the time of Pax Donald, the golden age
of the Gaeltachd, to the time of Our People. That is gone.
For most of us it is the same: we have family but no
people.

Only now, nearing the end, do I see that along the way
to the Loch of the Green Corrie, I have been finding my
people. Among the dead ones I number Norman and Sorley
himself, Crichton Smith, J. and Mal Duff and brave Don
Coppock. I number now among my people even those I
could never have met: AK MacLeod and Charlie Ross,
James Hutton and David Hume, stubborn Peach and Horne.
And those writers and singers and people who continue
to light up my life, who stand for something, whose words
cling inside my mind like scraps of wallpaper, layer on layer
– there is neither room nor need to list them here.

The circle expands across the lochan, wider and wider.

With Norman standing on my left, glass in one hand, fag in the other, I can finally face Sorley across the years and say 'These are my people.'

I moved along the shoreline, feeling as though some pilgrimage were nearly done; the book, if not the writing of it, is coming to its end. A fish caught here would be a final, living exclamation mark.

None came, though I worked and worked at it till my wrist ached and the stabbing under my shoulder demanded paracetamol washed down with loch water. I had one last go, working a little inlet that my instinct said was the place.

Nothing. I was flogging a dead loch, or at least one that wouldn't wake for me. MacCaig and his friends may well have caught *trout and invisible treasures* here; I'd have to settle for invisible trout.

So I stuffed landing net and flask into the pack, shouldered Peter's rod and set off back across the bog-scarred bealach. The afternoon was wearing late, the sky darkening. Down and across the moor lay another loch which my map identified as Loch Dubh Meallan Mhurchaidh. Bit of a mouthful – Sorley MacLean could have taken half a minute to sound it out – and I knew nothing about its potential.

But the slope beyond it glowed green and rust-red as if lit from below, and I went off in that direction, suddenly buoyant and light-footed.

Hard now to say how many years ago it was, but I was living alone in Queensferry, struggling for emotional self-

sufficiency with two cats for company. I was hurrying home
from the chip shop on a wintry night, cold wind, rain
mixed with spray from the estuary, collar up, hat down. Past
the yellow street lights, the fish supper warm on my palm
in my coat pocket, smelling the sharp vinegar. Then in the
wind came a great elation, and the words *When I am dead,
I will love this*.

Hunger with hot food in hand, wet night with street
lights and warm coat, home a few hundred yards distant –
this was earthly heaven, so right, so brief, so real.

It is what Norman and AK MacLeod, looking down
from the place they do not believe in, would give anything
for – one more day of catching or not catching fish at any
lochan. Fish supper warm in the hand on a cold wet night,
heading home hungry – nothing beats this, nothing. This
is what the dead envy us, the sweetness at the heart of
physical existence.

Pick any ordinary moment: arriving at a bus stop or
lochside, or sitting reading about a man going fishing – you
will love it when you're dead, so you can love it now.

As the book nears its end, and the wind drops behind
Canisp, I make a vow: from here on, all my awareness of
death and transience, of gone friends, family and lovers, the
past itself, must serve the cause of living.

Refreshed, reinvigorated for a while – no way will I be
able to be constant to that vow, but I'm damn well going
to try – I came down to the shore of Loch Dubh Meallan
Mhurchaidh, 'the black loch of Murchadh's Hillock'.

★

In the patch of sunlight I dropped the pack, ate the last of the chocolate – sweetness, passing sweetness! – and inspected the shoreline. The water was dark brown yet clear, perhaps it got deeper sooner than the last loch.

Why not? I cut off the Black Pennel that had lured nothing, opened my fly box and noticed, set slightly aside from the other lures, fakes, imitations and metaphors, the little plain brown thing Ian had given me at Torlundy a fortnight back. 'Dinni ken whit it's called,' he said, 'but it's caught mony a fish for me.'

I tied it on the bob dropper, the one nearest to me, and wearily, cheerfully stood up. I saw my reflection making ready to cast, and abruptly I was back by Loch Glascarnoch where I'd stopped on my first drive to Ullapool. The absolute stillness of that water, seeing the mountain Tom Ban Mor twice, the version going up and the one spread my way.

Outer world and inner world, the world doubled and made ambivalent, for it is easy to mistake one for the other though both are real. The two worlds hinge at the shoreline where MacCaig's poetry stands. Where any one of us stands.

Lures wetted, I began fishing my last loch of the day.

I was casting from a small headland, the water some eight feet below, when the line jerked. I flicked the rod tip up and the fish stayed on. The line spasmed to one side and another, burned over my finger. I pulled in quickly, thinking fast. Difficult to scramble down to the water with the landing net, and I could break Peter's rod or turn my ankle trying. Anyway the slack line would let the trout escape.

Nothing for it but to hoist the fish bodily from the water, up onto the bank.

Very common to lose it that way, and I so nearly did. It fell from Ian's hook – I have just mistyped 'book' – into the heather and lay spasming. As I grabbed the landing net, I heard it gasping, a small hoarse groping for life. Briefly it was in my hand, cool, slippery, muscular, yellow-silver-brown, open-mouthed. Not big, not small, under a pound. Then into the landing net with it.

I dropped the rod, slithered down the bank with the landing net to get the poor thing in the water. It jerked and twisted in the netting while I fumbled for the camera with my free hand. The photo seemed to matter, would be the last act of catching. And be some sort of proof – after all, I have been known to write fiction. I needed it to convince other people. I think I needed it to convince myself.

Two quick shots, the fish indiscernible in the netting. I took a chance and grabbed the twitching fish back out of the net with my left hand, held it at arm's length and took the picture with my right. Then back into the net, net lowered into the water.

I'd long wondered what to do when I caught my fish. Kill and eat it, as AK and Norman would have done? Our failure to cook Peter's fish still shamed us. Or better karma to let it go?

The moment that fish had fallen from the hook into the

heather, its fate was clear. I lowered the handle of the landing net, got one hand under and gave the wild brownie a lift. It flexed once and was gone.

'Thank you,' I said aloud as I stood on the bank. Thank you to many people, to this place. Bloody hell, I caught it.

I heard Norman say something dry in Latin – Catullus, I think – to the effect that despite what kindly women say, size does matter. That was not a big fish.

But hey, I did my best. I sat and laughed, shook my head as I do when something turns out right after all. This wasn't the Loch of the Green Corrie, nor was it Norman's 'Rich day' loch. It was one of my own.

I sat on my pack, looked out over the loch, then behind me at Canisp, and let the feeling sink in.

The wind had dropped completely, and a fish plopped heavily near the far bank. Then another, nearer. I should get up and try to catch more.

I sat and watched one fish after another rise and fall back. I let them be. The first one is fishing; after that it is just catching. A real fisherman would make the most of this; Norman and AK would compete with loving, intricate insults. But in the end I am not them. I am just myself, my shoulder aches and I feel happy, tired and oddly empty. Satisfied, you might say.

Caught and released, I got stiffly to my feet, and began to unpick the cast from the line.

★

It is time to dismantle the rod, close the book, shoulder whatever remains. We all have hungers and appetites, things to do, people to see, sleep to catch.

What remains is the descent. The rushing outflow burn, the broken moorland and the ancient bedrock, the darkening sky above Assynt and those bright lochans already passing from sight into memory, are what is left to us. Let it be enough.

Tired, enriched, unburdened for now, I follow the burn over the bealach and off the page, into where whatever has existed once, exists all the time.

The ten minutes are up, except they aren't.
I leave the village, except I don't.
The jig fades to silence, except it doesn't.

The Loch of the Green Corrie

(for Norman MacCaig)

We came to know it, a little.

It kept its best fish hidden
under glassy water, behind silver backing
of the long day's clouds.

We cast and retrieved by that mirror
till the Green Corrie reflected only
three bodies of light,

filling and emptying themselves.
That place hooked us by the heart.
We were landed and released.

Now something of us reclines among those hills
and the chuckle of its water
runs among the world.

READING

Stephen Baxter: *Revolutions in the Earth* (Weidenfeld & Nicolson 2003)

Peter Dorward: *Nightingale* (Two Ravens Press 2007)

Jay Griffiths: *Wild* (Penguin 2008)

Joy Hendry and Raymond Ross (editors): *Norman MacCaig: Critical Essays* (EUP 1990)

James Hunter: *The Claim of Crofting* (Edinburgh 1991), and other articles and lectures

John MacAskill: *We Have Won the Land* (Acair 1999)

Robert Macfarlane: *Mountains of the Mind* and *The Wild Places* (Granta Books 2008)

Allan Macinnes: *Clanship, Commerce and the House of Stuart* (Tuckwell Press 1996), and other essays and articles

Cathel MacLeod: *Trout Fishing in Assynt* (for this wonderful booklet guide, which includes the Loch of the Green Corrie, contact Achins Bookshop, Inverkirkaig)

Marjory McNeil: *Norman MacCaig: A Study of His Life and Work* (Mercat Press 1996)

Jack Rebcheck: *The Man Who Found Time* (Pocket Books 2004)

Edward Said: *On Late Style* (Bloomsbury 1996)

Nan Shepherd: *The Living Mountain* (Canongate Classics, 2001)

British Geological Survey: 'Scotland Special Sheet: Assynt: bedrock' 2007

ACKNOWLEDGEMENTS

I have many people to thank for their help, guidance, friendship, hospitality, trust, time and stories. These include: Angus John McEwan, Cathel MacLeod, Mandy Haggith and Bill Ritchie, Wilma Mackay, Wilma Macaskill, Alex at Achins Bookshop, The Assynt Foundation and Mark at Glencanisp Lodge, Rhona Mackenzie at Suil-na-Mara, David Greig for keeping me straight on the geology, Kevin MacNeil for Gaelic assist, John Aberdein and Lesley for their critical and creative reading. I am also indebted to Jon Riley and Charlotte Clerk at Quercus for their persistence, belief and clarity in helping shape this book.

To my companions in Assynt, Andrew and Peter Dorward, true fishermen and friends – my lasting gratitude for those days and many others.

A brief narrative of our Assynt trip appeared in *The Way to Cold Mountain*, ed. Alec Finlay, Pocketbooks 2001.
'Dub' appears in *A Wilder Vein*, ed. Linda Cracknell, Two Ravens Press 2009.
'First cast at the Loch of the Green Corrie' appears in *Powerlines: New Writing from the Water's Edge*, ed. Dexter Petley, Two Ravens Press 2009.

'Part the clouds, let me look down' is from Edwin Morgan's 'Jack London in Heaven'.

The John Berryman quote is from his *Dream Song 16*.

'Work of sight is achieved . . .' is from Rilke's *Turning*, trans. J.B. Leishman.

The Norman MacCaig poems reproduced here by kind permission, appear in *The Poems of Norman MacCaig:* (Polygon, 2005).

'In Praise of Assynt' was written by Angus John McEwan.

'Freedom Come All Ye' is by Hamish Henderson.

A version of 'A Scots Pine' appeared in the *New Edinburgh Review No. 126, 'Passing Places'*.

The photos come by kind permission of Peter and Andrew Dorward, Angus John McEwan, Wilma Mackay and William Macaskill.

Norman MacCaig acknowledged his own 'streak of reticence'. His son and daughter have decided to respect this and their contribution to this book has been limited to some assistance with key facts.